Gunter Steinmann
Ralf E. Ulrich (Eds.)

The Economic Consequences of Immigration to Germany

With 20 Figures and 34 Tables

Physica-Verlag
A Springer-Verlag Company

Professor Dr. Gunter Steinmann
Department of Economics
University of Halle-Wittenberg
Große Steinstr. 73
D-06108 Halle, FRG

Dr. Ralf E. Ulrich
Faculty of Social Sciences
Humboldt-University of Berlin
Unter den Linden 6
D-10099 Berlin, FRG

ISBN 3-7908-0796-6 Physica-Verlag Heidelberg

This work is subject to copyright. All rights are reserved, whether the whole or part of the material is concerned, specifically the rights of translation, reprinting, reuse of illustration, recitation, broadcasting, reproduction on microfilms or in other ways, and storage in data banks. Duplication of this publication or parts thereof is only permitted under the provisions of the German Copyright Law of September 9, 1965, in its version of June 24, 1985, and a copyright fee must always be paid. Violations fall under the prosecution act of the German Copyright Law.

© Physica-Verlag Heidelberg 1994
Printed in Germany

The use of registered names, trademarks, etc. in this publication does not imply, even in the absence of a specific statement, that such names are exempt from the relevant protective laws and regulations and therefore free for general use.

88/2202-543210 - Printed on acid-free paper

Introduction

This volume discusses some economic aspects of immigration with special reference to the case of Germany.

Immigration has become a major issue in Germany. Germany still does not have an official immigration policy in spite of the fact that more than 8 percent of the residents are non-citizens and that Germany´s immigration figures almost have reached the US figures.

The foreign labor supply strongly influences the German labor market. The bulk of foreign workers is employed in certain industries. In some industries (mining, steel) 20 and more percent of the employees are foreign workers. Most foreign workers are blue collar workers with low wages. The labor demand for immigrants has declined in the last 15 years while the foreign population and labor supply has increased. As a consequence, foreigners experience higher unemployment rates than Germans. The fall of the Berlin wall and the collapse of the communist regimes in East Europe further increased the blue collar labor supply and strengthened the competition for foreign workers on the German labor market.

There have been several periods of increased academic attention to immigration in Germany in the past. The economic and sociological studies of the early fifties dealt with the inflow of the millions of German refugees from East Europe. In the sixties the main interest was in the economic and social problems of guest workers from South Europe. When in 1973 the German government encouraged return migration of guest workers the emphasis of the studies shifted to problems of integrating the immigrants. Since the late eighties the consequences of increasing numbers of asylum seekers and of ethnic German immigrants from East Europe have become a main focus in the literature.

This book collects some recent works of German and American scholars dealing with economic aspects of immigration to Germany. *Christoph M. Schmidt* deals with two crucial questions: how will the migrants integrate into the existing labor force over time, and how will the migrant stream affect the wage and employment outcomes of native workers? He shows that Germany's own migration history yields data that could be used to answer these questions. Germany has already experienced permanent migration on a large scale, mainly through a change in the nature of guest worker migration in recent decades. *Schmidt* argues that the magnitude of migrant influx, the patterns of duration of stay, and location choices resemble the experience of typical immigration countries.

The future course of immigration to Germany will be influenced by its impact on national interest and wealth, by humanitarian considerations and by the ability of German institutions to regulate immigration. None of these factors can be safely predicted now. Some German scholars believe that the increased level of immigration as experienced in the past few years might be a model for a new era of immigration after the fall of the iron curtain. The paper of *Ralf E. Ulrich* tries to quantify what dimensions such a development would imply. Demographic projections are used to illustrate the long-term effects of two immigration scenarios under given mortality and fertility assumptions. *Ulrich* shows that if the current high level of immigration and the current naturalization regime were continued foreigners would reach a share of 30 percent of Germany's population within the next forty years. It is obvious that its institutions and people will have to adjust to a very different situation within a comparably short period.

Gunter Steinmann presents a theoretical model to analyse the economic effects of immigration on the income of natives. He shows that, in nearly all cases, natives will benefit from immigration in the long run, but that they will most likely be harmed in the short run. This is due to the "investment costs" (costs of integration) that natives are usually required to pay for some period of time to new immigrants. The assessment of immigrants' value, therefore, depends upon the time horizon of the natives.

The impact of immigration on public expenditures and revenues is among the key concerns in public opinion. *Ralf E. Ulrich* uses microdata from the German Socio-Economic Panel to estimate the net contribution of foreigners to the public coffer. He concludes that foreigners in the past decades until today paid more to the public households than they received. The main reason for this is their large net contribution to the pension system, due to their juvenile age structure. In the sixties there were also other reasons like a higher labor force participation, lower unemployment rate and lower absence from work due to illness. These factors gradually disappeared over the past decades. Given reasonable assumptions the foreign population in Germany will inevitably grow older. If the juvenile age structure loses its impact foreigners might become a net burden for Germany's public households in the future.

Native blue collar workers often fear the competition of foreigners, as they may induce declining wages and rising unemployment. This would have to be expected if natives and immigrants were substitutes. Substitutability might even be greater between foreign labor already in Germany and those newly arriving. The paper of *John P. De New* and *Klaus F. Zimmermann* outlines the issue in a framework with two types of labor, native blue collar and foreign blue collar. Examining the wage functions of blue collar natives and foreigners in a random effects panel model using a vast sample of micro data, they actually find that foreigners negatively affect the wages of Germans and themselves on the whole. Negative effects are experienced by blue collar employees with less than 20 years of experience, but these are outweighed by the much larger negative effects experienced by blue collar foreigners with more than 20 years of experience.

The German guest worker system was for decades characterized by the temporary nature of immigration. In the last decade this has changed. Foreigners increasingly consider their stay in Germany as permanent. The paper of *Viktor Steiner* and *Johannes Velling* analyzes guest workers' expected duration of stay in Germany within an econometric model taking into account the important distinction between permanent and temporary residents, where the expected duration of stay for the latter is differentiated in short-term, mid-term and long-term residents. The model is estimated for household heads with the first six waves of the German Socio-Economic Panel, taking advantage of the panel structure of our data base to obtain efficient parameter estimates.

Immigration is sometimes seen as a factor creating additional unemployment in the host country. In their paper *Ira N. Gang* and *Francisco L. Rivera-Batiz* examine the effects of the presence of foreigners on the employment status of native-born German citizens. It also analyzes the attitudes toward foreigners displayed by German individuals in various labor market situations. They do not find evidence that higher concentrations of foreign-born workers are correlated with greater unemployment among native-born residents. They do observe, however, that unemployed Germans perceive that there is a larger presence of foreigners in their neighborhood, when compared to the employed. In terms of attitudes towards foreigners, there seems to be no pattern linking unemployed Germans to a more negative attitude towards foreigners in general. On the other hand, the authors found evidence that the unemployed feel that particular groups of foreigners, such as Turks and North Africans, generate job losses for the native-born.

A unique group of immigrants to Germany are ethnic Germans from Eastern Europe. They have been called Vertriebene in the past and are called Aussiedler today. After World War II more than 10 million Vertriebene came to Germany. Their integration was one of the major achievements of post-war West Germany. On the other hand Vertriebene made an important contribution to the German "economic miracle" of the fifties. The paper of *Ralf E. Ulrich* compares the success story of the fifties with today's conditions and the experience with the integration of recent Aussiedler.

Contents

	Introduction	v
1	Immigration Countries and Migration Research: The Case of Germany *Christoph M. Schmidt*	1
2	The Future Growth of Foreign Population in Germany *Ralf E. Ulrich*	21
3	The Effects of Immigrants on the Income of Natives *Gunter Steinmann*	45
4	Foreigners and the Social Insurance System in Germany *Ralf E. Ulrich*	61
5	Blue Collar Labor Vulnerability: Wage Impacts of Migration *John P. De New and Klaus F. Zimmermann*	81
6	Re-Migration Behavior and Expected Duration of Stay of Guest Workers in Germany *Viktor Steiner and Johannes Velling*	101
7	Unemployment and Attitudes Towards Foreigners in Germany *Ira N. Gang and Francisco L. Rivera-Batiz*	121
8	Vertriebene and Aussiedler - The Immigration of Ethnic Germans *Ralf E. Ulrich*	155

Immigration Countries and Migration Research: The Case of Germany[1]

Christoph M. Schmidt
SELAPO, University of Munich, and CEPR, London
Ludwigstrasse 28 RG
80539 Munich, Germany

1 Introduction

The Federal Republic of Germany does not belong to the set of "classical" immigration countries like Australia, Canada or the United States. Nevertheless, migration has become a topic of increased interest for the whole of western Europe and, in particular, for Germany. This interest has arisen from the expectation of massive migration flows in the near future: migrants from the new democracies in East Europe, migrants moving within the growing European Community from the south to the north, and migrants trying to escape war and starvation in many countries of the Third World. It is believed that these flows will particularly affect Germany because of its ties to East Europe and its relative affluence.

A central issue of the migration discussion is the integration of incoming migrants into the labor force. At the present time, it is uncertain how the expected migrants will perform in the labor market. Will they consistently lag behind and become a burden to the welfare system, or will they become a viable part of the labor force and contribute to economic growth? It is also unclear which effects their presence will have on the labor market outcomes of native workers. Will natives suffer significant losses in wage earnings, and will they experience higher unemployment?

What can the results from existing international migration research contribute to the prediction of these migration effects? Virtually all of the existing evidence in this line of research has been generated for the United States or for other

---

[1] This paper is a revised version of "The Economic Consequences of International Migration: Status of International Research and Applications to the Federal Republic of Germany" that was written in February 1991 while the author was a graduate student at Princeton University. I gratefully acknowledge financial support from the Industrial Relations Section, Princeton University, and from the Alfred P. Sloan Foundation through its Doctoral Dissertation Fellowship. The paper benefitted from discussions with David Card, Ani Dasgupta, Christian Dustmann, Anette Gehrig, Franque Grimard, Annamaria Lusardi, Rolf Tschernig, Rainer Winkelmann and Klaus F. Zimmermann.

classical immigration countries. It reveals quite consistently that migrant earnings rise disproportionally quickly, and that native employment does not suffer significantly from migrant influx. But the labor market structure of these countries is so different from Germany's- pertaining to issues of job security, minimum wages, work characteristics and union representation- that unfortunately few results from these studies carry over directly to the German case. In particular, the menu of labor market outcomes that should be examined is different from, for example, the United States. The principal lessons for analyses of the German situation are thus arising from methodological deliberations. One of the major results of economic migration research has been that any sensible empirical treatment of the questions raised above requires an approach that explicitly deals with the quality mix among the migrant work force.

The German data available today describe mainly the labor market experiences of guest workers, while the questions arising from Germany's new role as an immigration country refer more to permanent migration. Thus, at first glance it appears doubtful that anything could be learned from a look at Germany's own migration history. Indeed, the current debate reflects these doubts. It focuses on a narrow subset of the problem: economically motivated migrants trying to enter Germany via its generous laws regarding political asylum. In essence, migration is treated as if it were a new problem to Germany. A closer look reveals, in contrast, that Germany's own migration experience could indeed be analyzed by empirical studies on the micro level. It is argued in this paper that Germany has, in fact, been an immigration country for several years. What started as the temporary migration of guest workers in the 1960s has gradually become permanent migration, as both the German economy developed and the origin of migrants changed. Parallels between Germany and other immigration countries, with regard to the nature of immigration can be drawn from the magnitude of the influx, the typical duration of stay and the patterns of location choice.

Section 2 of this paper describes the current developments in the international migration potential, and introduces the questions they raise for Germany. Section 3 presents some basic econometric models that have been employed in previous empirical analyses and discusses their applicability to Germany. Section 4 demonstrates that Germany's labor market history can be identified as that of an immigration country. The final section, section 5, is a conclusion.

2 The Future of Western Europe

Large population movements to Western Europe can be expected in the near future. These movements can be roughly categorized into three overlapping groups. First, the collapse of communism in Eastern Europe has led to the potential for a substantial East-West migration. Several Western European countries are apt to become targets of East European migrants. In all likelihood, Germany will be most affected, because of its geographical location and, paradoxically, because of its citizenship regulations. The acquisition of German citizenship is difficult and expensive. However, according to the German Ministry of Interior Affairs, about 3.7 million descendants of German settlers who located mainly in Czarist Russia are regarded as German citizens, and any limitations on their entry into Germany are precluded. Only upon economic equalization between the eastern and western European economies is the East-West migration flow likely to cease.

Second, the formal creation of a common European labor market as of January 1st, 1993, will allow all individuals falling under European jurisdiction to move freely within the Community. This will most likely lead to an intra-European migration flow from the Mediterranean basin to the northern countries of the EC. These movements will often be only temporary in character, and an assessment of their consequences is therefore very difficult. Since no legal restrictions between member states will preclude interregional mobility, one country could become the gateway to all other countries. The addition of new member states will probably cause an enlargement of the migration stream. New members from Eastern Europe will add to the East-West migration potential; new members from the South will add to the potential of South-North migration. Again, Germany will be most affected by this probable development. The integration of Turkey, for example, would likely lead to a large migration flow from Turkey to Germany, due mainly to existing cultural, family and informational ties.

Third, the wealthier countries of the world all face the potential for a huge migration flow from the Third World. While poverty, starvation, and the dangers of war and political oppression have plagued humanity in the past, several developments have made a growth of this potential for poverty-induced migration possible. One of these developments is the population growth in the Third World that is documented in Table 1. World population is expected to rise to 8.5 billion by 2025. Most of this growth will be coming from the less developed economies, whose population growth rates continue to increase relative to those of the developed economies. The availability of travel opportunities and decreasing information costs also contribute to the ability to leave a poor home country. Germany, as one of the richest countries in the world, cannot expect to be excluded as a target of migrant aspirations.

Table 1: Development of the World Population:
Levels ('000,000) and Growth Rates (%)

	World	Europe	Africa	America*	Asia	Australia & Oceania	developed +	less developed++
1950	2515	593	224	331	1354	13	-	-
	1.79	0.79	2.18	1.80, 2.81	1.90	2.25	1.28	2.05
1960	3019	667	281	416	1639	16	-	-
	1.99	0.91	2.48	1.49, 2.75	2.19	2.08	1.19	2.35
1970	3698	738	363	512	2066	19	-	-
	1.97	0.58	2.69	1.06, 2.32	2.27	1.78	0.86	2.39
1980	4450	794	481	614	2538	23	-	-
	1.74	0.32	2.95	1.00, 2.19	1.86	1.55	0.65	2.10
1985	4854	819	557	668	2784	25	-	-
	1.73	0.23	3.00	0.82, 2.07	1.85	1.44	0.53	2.10
1990	5292	841	648	724	3053	26	-	-
	1.71	0.22	3.01	0.71, 1.90	1.82	1.33	0.48	2.06
2000	6251	883	872	835	3631	30	-	-
	1.47	0.13	2.84	0.56, 1.59	1.44	1.18	0.38	1.74
2010	7191	917	1148	942	4149	34	-	-
	1.21	0.02	2.42	0.52, 1.35	1.09	1.04	0.27	1.41
2025	8467	953	1581	1093	4800	39	-	-
	0.98	-0.06	1.85	0.35, 1.10	0.87	0.85	0.18	1.13

Source: Statistisches Bundesamt. Growth rates are calculated as averages for the subsequent 5-year intervals, except for 2025 which shows the average growth rate for 2020 to 2025. Starting with 1990 levels and starting with 1985 growth rates are predicted by the United Nations (medium variant).
* The first growth rate refers to North America, the second to South America
+ Europe (including the Soviet Union), North America, Japan, Australia and New Zealand
++ Africa, Latin America, East and South Asia and Oceania

Table 2 compares Germany to other potential destination countries - the members of the European Community, the United States and Japan - in 1988 with respect to age composition, earnings and employment opportunities. Germany already has the highest percentage of population over age 45. This fact displays the ageing of the German work force, which seems to have generated an increased demand for young migrant labor. Abstracting from Luxemburg, Germany is also very attractive for potential migrants in terms of relative labor market outcomes. It is second behind the United States in hourly wages, and its unemployment rate falls into the bottom half of all unemployment rates of the EC countries. In addition, Germany offers a tight-knit social net that might also attract immigrants.

Table 2: Age Composition, Hourly Wages and Unemployment Rates
The European Community, the United States and Japan 1988

	Over Age 45 (%)	Hourly Wage (DM)	Unemployment Rate (%)
Germany	41.4	18.49	8.7
Belgium	37.4	15.63	11.1
Denmark	37.1	16.68	8.4
France	34.8	12.35	10.9
Greece	38.4	6.64	7.4
UK	37.0	13.44	8.5
Ireland	28.0	11.96	18.6
Italy	38.0	-	16.4
Luxemburg	37.2	21.42	1.6
The Netherlands	33.0	16.50	7.4
Portugal	34.2	3.98	6.7
Spain	34.5	10.36	19.9
United States	31.0	18.65	5.4
Japan	36.2	11.06	2.5

Source: Statistisches Bundesamt, own calculations

The ensuing migration streams will have economic consequences for the migrants themselves, on the one hand, and for both the natives remaining in the country of origin and the natives in the destination country, on the other hand. From the perspective of an immigration country, the effects on the first and the third group of individuals are of interest. The labor market performance of immigrants is determined both by the characteristics of the individuals that decide to migrate and by the way these characteristics are valued in the labor market of the host country. It seems only natural that migrants initially earn less than natives, since many aspects of the new labor market are unknown to them. But how fast are they able to close this initial gap? It is this movement that economists concentrate on when they talk about immigrant assimilation. The answer to this question might determine the future of the economy as a whole. To the extent that individuals at the lower end of the earnings distribution have a high risk of unemployment, and to the extent that economic growth depends mainly upon the availability of skilled workers, one can argue that there is a relationship between the degree of assimilation and the aggregate effects of a given stream of immigrants.

In addition, natives have traditionally been very concerned with the magnitude of the immigrant stream; there is an underlying fear that immigrant labor tends to lower the wage level and crowd out native labor. Clearly, an appropriate answer to this question first has to identify the subset of natives that could potentially be displaced by immigrant workers and then has to determine the correct substitution elasticities. Since, at first glance, Germany's own migration experience has been confined mainly to guest workers, one cannot directly infer either on the labor market outcomes this new, permanent type of migrants will achieve or the effects these migrants will have on native labor. The next section reviews several approaches that have been taken in empirical migration research and discusses the direct transferability of their results to the case of Germany.

3 Empirical Analyses of the Impact of Migration

What can international migration research reveal (for an overview see Borjas, 1990)? If the set of immigrants possessed the mix of characteristics of the native work force in the host country, a modelling approach which assumes labor to be a homogeneous production factor could be a promising avenue. A given number of migrants would then simply result in an outward shift in both the labor supply schedule and the goods demand schedule, in a general equilibrium framework. This is the perspective that many theoretical studies of migration take. Most aggregate analyses of international migration flows model labor markets as competitive and conclude that immigration is enhancing the welfare of incumbent native workers (a classic paper is Berry and Soligo, 1969). In contrast, studies that focus on the problem of rural to urban migration in developing countries generally view migration as exacerbating already existing unemployment in the receiving area (most of this work originated in Harris and Todaro, 1970).

It has been a common observation of empirical studies, however, that migrants' characteristics tend to be distinctly different from those of natives. Consequently, there is a large body of literature that recognizes migrant heterogeneity and concentrates on the micro level. Studies of growth in the earnings of immigrant workers have been done mainly for the United States (seminal papers are Chiswick, 1978, and Borjas, 1987; for Germany see Dustmann, 1993, Licht and Steiner, 1993, Pischke, 1992, or Schmidt, 1992a and 1992b). The typical approach to estimation is to postulate a linear functional relationship between the logarithm of individual earnings and exogenous explanatory factors collected in a vector X. Interest in the migration literature has focused on differences in the way earnings of immigrants have been rising over the duration of stay in the host country, τ, in comparison to the earnings of natives, when differences in other explanatory variables have been controlled for. The earnings of individual i are then given by:

$$\ln w_i = X'_i \beta + \delta_0 * foreign_i + \delta_1 * \tau_i * foreign_i + e_i$$

where *foreign$_i$* is an indicator that is unity for migrants and zero otherwise. The initial gap between the wages of immigrants and those of native workers is generally represented by a large negative value of δ_0. The degree to which immigrants succeed to narrow, or even close the initial wage gap is measured by the difference in growth rates of the earnings of the two groups of workers, represented in the regression by δ_1.

It is viewed as an unambiguous fact that the initial wage gap is closed to a certain degree in the years following immigration. Cross-sectional earnings profiles indeed suggest that immigrants are able to catch up to native wages after less than two decades in the labor market. In attempts to explain this finding, it is often argued (this argument originated in Chiswick, 1978) that migrants are not a randomly selected sample of the population in the country of origin, but rather that they are positively selected. The decision to migrate requires extraordinary motivation and courage, and thus high quality workers tend to move, while those of lower quality stay behind. However, difficulties in distinguishing true behavioral effects from problems of measurement have led to an unsolved controversy in the empirical migration literature. These problems are potentially important for any empirical analysis of German data.

The static model developed by Roy (1951), and most prominently used in migration research by Borjas (1987), is able to capture the essence of this debate. Originally developed to describe occupational choice, the Roy model simultaneously models the migration decision and the labor market outcome for migrants in a full-employment world. Crucial for the migration decision in the Roy model is the potential earnings difference between (log) earnings in the source country, $ln\ w_{0i}$, and (log) earnings in the host country, $ln\ w_{1i}$, net of the cost of migration. Both individual earnings opportunities in the two countries and cost of migration differ among individuals. This individual heterogeneity is expressed in the model by the presence of individual deviation terms u_{0i} and u_{1i} from average earnings μ_0 and μ_1, respectively:

$$lnw_{0i} = \mu_0 + u_{0i}$$
$$lnw_{1i} = \mu_1 + u_{1i}$$

A bivariate normal distribution of these random variables reflects the income distribution that one would expect if all potential migrants chose to live in the given location. A given individual i decides to migrate if his or her earnings in the destination country will exceed those in the source country,

$$u_{1i} - u_{0i} > \mu_0 - \mu_1.$$

Consequently, the pool of migrants will be self-selected according to the realization of the unobservables. Depending on the specific configuration of the model parameters, three different scenarios could characterize the type of migration that will be observed. Migrants could, on average, be those individuals doing particularly well in both countries, those doing particularly poorly in both countries, or finally, those doing poorly in the home country but well in the destination country. The character of selection is, therefore, determined by the dispersion of earnings and by the correlation between the individual outcomes in the two countries.

In light of this model, it can be discussed why several economists do not view the apparent assimilation as genuine but instead as a statistical artifact. In cross-sectional studies, the behavior of the earnings of workers over their life-cycles was inferred from the earnings of comparable individuals who were at different points in their lives at the time the cross-section was collected. This approach opens the door to two major econometric problems concerned with the self-selection of the observed cross-sectional sample according to unobserved variables: first, self-selection at the time of entry into the host country and second, re-emigration according to the realization of economic success or failure in the host country. The main empirical argument is that the distribution of unobservables may change substantially over time. If, in particular, the unobservable quality characteristics of entering immigrant cohorts decreases over time, then a cross-section of migrants will contain "better" migrants who stayed in the host country for a long time and "worse" migrants whose duration of stay was short. These unobservable quality differences will lead to a difference in average earnings that the researcher might falsely attribute to assimilation.

The sorting due to re-emigration biases the results of cross-sectional studies for similar reasons (a theoretical model of this sorting process is given by McCall and McCall, 1987). In the case of the United States, the typical individual re-emigrating to his source country is likely to have experienced a relatively unsuccessful period in the United States labor market. Most immigrants coming to the United States do not intend to work there for only a limited period of time but instead intend to stay permanently. Therefore, the bulk of re-emigrants are individuals who had reasons to revise their future plans after they entered the United States. As an empirical consequence, the sample of immigrants who stayed in their host country for a number of years is not a random sub-sample of those individuals who entered initially. Indeed, the remaining sample will possess a mix of observed and unobserved individual characteristics of increasing average quality, and again the researcher might falsely attribute differences in earnings to assimilation effects.

The discussion of both of these problems is of great importance for the interpretation of German evidence. The origin of immigrant flows has changed over time and, therefore, so will have the distribution of unobservable migrant characteristics. If guest workers generally stay for a predetermined time in their host country, re-migration will not create econometric problems for German data. If, instead, there is a strong link between return to the home country and economic success for guest workers, the problem of econometrically accounting for re-emigrants may be important. In any case, the results derived from United States data cannot be directly transferred to Germany.

In contrast to research on the labor market performance of immigrants, the existing analyses of the effects of immigration on native labor focus not only on earnings but on employment as well. The basic questions are whether immigrant labor tends to be a close substitute for native labor and to which degree native wages are undercut by immigrants. These issues are difficult to address on an aggregate level, since the aggregate movements of wages and employment are influenced simultaneously by a variety of factors, and only one realization of the process is available. Existing work, therefore, tends to focus on the behavior of regional or local native labor market outcomes with relation to the regional variation of the density of the immigrant population (see for example Card, 1990, Altonji and Card, 1990, and Butcher and Card, 1991). Immigrant labor in these models is generally viewed as an outward shift in local or regional labor supply; the models are distinguished mainly by the degree to which immigrants have an effect on demand in goods markets. Empirically, one way to proceed involves two regression steps. In the first step individual measures of native employment performance - wages, weeks worked per year, labor force participation rates - in different regions are corrected for composition effects in order to form composition-adjusted regional measures. In the second step, these adjusted regional measures are explained by a number of regional characteristics, in particular the ratio of immigrants to population.

Research along these lines does not find evidence for a substantial effect of the size of the immigrant population on native labor market outcomes. For Germany, with its institutionalized collective bargaining structure, the process of wage and employment determination is different than that of the United States. In particular, if the number of native workers forced into unemployment is increased dramatically by immigrant workers, native workers or their union representatives might have a strong interest in the restriction of the immigration flow. One reason for the small number of studies addressing this subject is the need for regionally segmented labor markets. In the United States, data on this type of market is provided by the distinction of Standardized Metropolitan Statistical Areas (SMSA). Such a regional structure cannot be observed in European countries. Thus, the results of analyses of United States data can again be only imperfectly transferred to Germany.

We may be unable to translate these results directly to the German labor market for another, more fundamental reason. One could argue that permanent migration on a large scale has not been experienced by the German economy in the past, because most of the immigration has been of temporary character. Consequently, the reaction of the German labor market to the influx of permanent labor could not be inferred from previous experience. The next section will review the German immigration experience, and will argue instead that permanent migration has, in the past, already been an important form of migration into Germany.

4 Migration and the German Labor Market

According to a popular view, Germany is not an immigration country. Immigration countries are expected to open their borders to foreigners who want to settle permanently in their host country only under explicit conditions. The migration policies of the prototypical immigration countries, the United States, Canada and Australia, have shaped this view. These countries select migrants according to individual criteria or according to quota and they allow the chosen migrants to acquire their respective citizenship. This strategy enables immigrants to melt with the already existing population into a common whole. In particular, it provides for the possibility of an active immigrant participation in the political decision process.

In essence, the behavior of these three countries is regarded as a necessary condition for being awarded the status "immigration country", and migration is treated as a problem of legal definitions. The current political debate is a manifestation of this position. Facing the immigration pressures described in section 2 and the large number of economically motivated migrants trying to enter Germany via its generous laws regarding political asylum, it is currently being discussed whether Germany should become an immigration country through a change in its immigration regulations.

From an economist's point of view, this discussion is empty. With particular regard to the labor market consequences that are the focus of this paper, citizenship regulations are all but irrelevant. Migration is simply the relocation of individuals across jurisdictional and/or geographical boundaries, irrespective of a government's position towards incoming migrants. What, then, constitutes a typical immigration country? Clearly, this must be defined by actual migration streams rather than by the policies towards these migrants. Many detailed definitions are possible, but they all should contain some or all of the elements to be discussed below.

First, an immigration country should receive a large stream of immigrants, consistently over a considerable period of time, i.e, large gross immigration. Which numbers could be defined as "large" could be measured both in absolute terms and/or in relation to the native population. Straubhaar and Zimmermann (1991) and Schmidt and Zimmermann (1992) argue for gross immigration as the decisive measure of the integration cost levied on a host country. On the basis of this measure, they further argue that Germany has been an immigration country for a long time. Second, an immigration country should consistently experience a net influx, i.e. a positive and considerably large stream of net immigration. It is demonstrated in Schmidt and Zimmermann (1992) that apart from the years 1967, 1974-1976 and 1982-1984 net immigration into Germany has been positive and substantial.

Third, the patterns of duration of stay are important. Basically, a large proportion of the migrants into an immigration country are expected to stay for a considerably long time. That is, there should be a large number of permanent migrants. The apparent confinement of Germany's immigration experience to temporary migrants, the guest workers, could be cited as a basic reason for not defining Germany as an immigration country. What duration of stay in the host country is deemed sufficient for a person to be considered a permanent migrant depends largely on the questions the researcher wants to answer. From a labor market perspective, it is secondary whether retirees spend their pensions in their country of origin or in their host country. I will indeed argue below that, in fact, a large fraction of immigration into Germany has been permanent.

There are several characteristics that are usually typical for immigration countries. Among these are high growth, low fertility, low unemployment, low inflation and easily available information about economic conditions. While these conditions are largely responsible for the existence and the size of the immigration stream, they fail to define an immigration country as much as the focus on legal distinctions has failed to define it. A typical example would be Israel. Many emigrants from the Soviet Union move to Israel solely for religious reasons. If this stream were large, Israel could be an immigration country even if all the characteristics listed above were not satisfied.

The following paragraphs will discuss the importance of migrant influx and immigrants' patterns of duration of stay for Germany. From a historical perspective, it has been well documented who has entered Germany in the years since its foundation (see Straubhaar and Zimmermann, 1991, Franz, 1991, or Schmidt and Zimmermann, 1992). Relatively large streams of immigrants entered Germany, for a variety of reasons and from various origins. Henceforth, all figures will apply to the Federal Republic of Germany before German re-unification.

Table 3 documents the major immigrant flows into Germany in the last decade. *Aussiedler* are Germans originating in Eastern or South-Eastern Europe who are repatriated in Germany. *Übersiedler* are Germans who left East Germany (the German Democratic Republic, GDR) or East-Berlin in order to settle in the Federal Republic of Germany. German immigration laws have always been very restrictive, but permanent immigration has been possible for these two groups of individuals. Before 1987, however, none of these groups created an influx exceeding 40,000 individuals per year, due to the restrictions imposed by the Communist governments in their countries of origin. Only over the last few years has the number of migrants from Eastern Block countries been steadily rising. This development of East-West migration reached its climax in the turbulent months around the tumbling of the Berlin Wall. Although most of these individuals had been German citizens by definition, with regard to their participation in the labor market they have to be viewed as migrants. Both their cultural background and education, and their previous labor market experience have been acquired in another country and/or economic system. With German unification, the migrant category of Übersiedler ceased to exist.

While these flows have been relatively small, already having started in the 1950s, large numbers of guest workers, mainly from Southern Europe, pursued their version of a "German dream". In general, both the guest workers and their children who were born in Germany are not awarded German citizenship. Many foreigners satisfy the basic eligibility requirements for German citizenship, such as considerable duration of stay and language proficiency. Nevertheless, the number of new citizenships per year is in the magnitude of a tenth of the influx of foreign immigrants, and many long-term migrants remain foreigners. Thus, I will concentrate on statistically describing "foreigners" instead of "foreign born".

Table 3: Immigrant Flows, Federal Republic of Germany 1980-1989 ('000)

	1980	1981	1982	1983	1984	1985	1986	1987	1988	1989
Aussiedler		1968 - 1983: 616.4			36.5	39.0	42.8	78.5	202.7	377.1
Übersiedler	12.0	14.5	12.8	10.7	38.7	26.3	26.2	19.0	39.8	343.9
Foreigners:										
Gross Influx	631.4	501.1	321.7	272.3	331.1	398.2	479.5	473.1	648.6	770.8
Asylum Seekers	107.8	49.4	37.4	19.7	35.3	73.8	99.7	57.4	103.1	121.3
Net Influx	245.6	85.6	-111.6	-151.6	-213.9	31.5	131.5	139.0	289.5	332.5

Source: Statistisches Bundesamt, Institut der deutschen Wirtschaft

A massive influx from the Mediterranean basin was triggered by the active recruitment policy of the German government that started in 1955 and was intensified after the Berlin Wall was built in 1961 (see Schmidt and Zimmermann, 1992). Over time, the origin of guest worker immigration changed. Originally, the greatest guest worker supply was provided by Italy, later by Yugoslavia, and more recently by Turkey. In 1973, the recruitment was brought to a halt as a measure against the steadily rising unemployment in Germany. This policy is still in force. After a short recession of the influx and a corresponding rise in the emigration of foreigners, influx stabilized again at several hundred thousand individuals per year. This open circumvention of the declared anti-immigration policy has been possible mainly through family reunions. Only recently has the number of applicants for political asylum represented a large proportion of the gross influx of immigrants.

The development over the last decade is documented in Table 3. In total, Germany has experienced both a large gross influx and, on average, considerable net immigration. Note that net immigration is much smaller than the gross figures. Thus, it seems that temporary migration was the preferred mode in Germany. However, I will demonstrate below how, over time, the character of guest worker immigration more closely resembled that experienced by one of the typical immigration countries.

Table 4: Population, Foreigners and the Work Force ('000,000) in the Federal Republic of Germany 1960 - 1987

Year	Population			Work Force				Unemployment Rat	
	All	Foreign	Foreign %	All	Partici-pation, %	Foreign	Partici-pation, %	All %	Foreign %
1960	55.43	-	-	26.52	47.8	-	-	-	-
1965	58.62	-	-	27.03	46.1	1.22	-	0.7	0.2
1970	60.65	2.98	4.9	26.82	44.2	1.95	65.4	0.7	0.3
1975	61.83	4.09	6.6	26.88	43.5	2.19	53.5	4.7	6.8
1980	61.57	4.45	7.2	27.22	44.2	2.12	47.6	3.8	5.0
1985	61.02	4.38	7.2	27.85	45.6	1.84	42.0	9.3	13.9
1987	61.08	4.24	6.9	28.99	47.5	1.88	44.3	8.9	14.3

Source: Institut der deutschen Wirtschaft, own calculations

The German work force increased steadily from 26.5 million in 1960 to 29 million in 1987, and foreign workers had a substantial share in this growth. Table 4 shows the development of the native and foreign *populations* and of the *work force* between 1960 and 1987. It can be clearly seen that the size of the native population has decreased in the last two decades, while the number of foreigners grew in the early 1970s and, until today, has stayed at a level of over 4 million. Over the same time span the number of foreigners participating in the labor market, after a short increase, gradually fell below the level of 1970. Labor force participation rates of foreigners, which had been as high as 65%, dropped even below those of natives. The usual problems in determining reliable estimates of unemployment rates and labor force participation rates from administrational data arise in this context *a fortiori*: Foreigners who do not register as unemployed due to lack of eligibility for unemployment support may be actively looking for work, and, on the other hand, foreigners who intend to return to their country may register as unemployed to collect insurance benefits.

This already indicates that foreigners began to resemble the native population in several important respects. While the prototypical guest worker of the 1960s may have been a single male worker who moved to his home country after a temporary assignment, guest workers in later decades settled in Germany on a more permanent basis. This is also documented in the *unemployment* rates tabulated in Table 4. Unemployment rates among foreigners began to rise substantially above those of native workers in the 1970s. A large part of this difference might be due to composition effects. If foreign workers tend to be of comparatively low skill and if unemployment hits unskilled labor harder than skilled labor, then the unemployment rate among foreigners should be relatively high. Nevertheless, this indicates that returning to the home country was an option that many unemployed guest workers did not exercise. Germany's generous system of unemployment insurance may have contributed to this phenomenon.

Table 5: Foreign Employees in Germany 1955-1989 ('000)
(Sozialversicherungspflichtig beschäftigte Ausländer)

Year	Employed All	Foreign, %	Turkish, %	Yugos-lavian, %	Ethnic Composition Italian, %	Greek, %	Spanish, %	Portu-guese, %
1955	20000.0	80.0	-	-	7.5	0.6	0.5	-
		0.4	-	-	9.4	0.8	0.6	-
1960	21933.3	329.0	3.0	9.0	144.0	21.0	16.0	0.3
		1.5	0.9	2.7	43.8	6.4	4.9	0.1
1965	21350.9	1217.0	133.0	64.0	372.0	187.0	183.0	14.0
		5.7	10.9	5.3	30.6	15.4	15.0	1.2
1970	21417.6	1949.0	354.0	423.0	382.0	242.0	172.0	45.0
		9.1	18.2	21.7	19.6	12.4	8.8	2.3
1975	20188.1	2039.0	543.0	416.0	292.0	196.0	125.0	68.0
		10.1	26.6	20.4	14.3	9.6	6.1	3.3
1980	21221.1	2016.0	588.0	349.0	308.0	130.0	85.0	58.0
		9.5	29.2	17.3	15.3	6.4	4.2	2.9
1985	20881.6	1587.0	503.4	295.4	198.4	102.0	67.2	35.3
		7.6	31.7	18.6	12.5	6.4	4.2	2.2
1989	21657.9	1646.0	552.4	295.1	173.6	98.7	61.7	38.2
		7.6	33.6	17.9	10.5	6.0	3.7	2.3

Source: Institut der deutschen Wirtschaft, own calculations

Table 5 summarizes the evolution of *employment* from 1955 to 1989. Foreign employment reached its peak in the 1970s and subsequently did not drop below 7.5% of total employment. Thus, even in the 1980s foreigners remained an integral part of employment, despite the persistently high unemployment rates. This table also shows how the composition of foreign workers, according to their country of origin, changed over time. Italians were the predominant group until the late 1960s, with a share of foreign employment as high as 44% in 1960. From the middle of the 1970s guest workers from Turkey have had the largest share of foreign employment, currently about one third. It is also apparent from this table that, abstracting from the small Portuguese community, employment for all large ethnic groups other than Turkish workers peaked between 1965 and 1970 and has markedly dropped since. Turkish employment peaked at roughly 600,000 in 1980 and has since remained at over half a million.

As stated in Table 6, the average duration of stay of guest workers appears to have risen dramatically over time. In 1977 about a quarter of the foreigners had entered Germany at least ten years ago. This number rose to about 60% by 1986. From the information on elapsed durations of stay in the host country one can attempt to recover the distribution of completed durations of stay. Any researcher who tries to infer on guest workers' return propensities by fitting separate discrete time constant hazard models to the data given at each of the ten sampling points, respectively, would estimate an average completed duration of stay of 8.9 years in 1977. This figure would rise monotonically over time; in 1986 the estimated completed duration of stay would be 19.9 years.

Table 6: Foreigners in Germany ('000): Time Since First Entry 1977-1986

Date	Overall	<1 Year, %	1-4 Years, %	4-6 Years, %	6-8 Years, %	8-10 Years, %	>10 Years, %	Implied Mean Duration, Years	
30.9.77+	3949.3	210.3	672.1	695.6	750.9	494.1	877.2	8.9	14.2
		5.3	17.0	17.6	19.0	12.5	22.2		
30.9.78+	3981.1	218.8	592.7	617.5	640.7	696.3	985.0	9.6	14.9
		5.5	14.9	15.5	16.1	17.5	24.7		
30.9.79+	4143.8	250.0	611.7	438.0	644.6	701.5	1254.3	10.8	16.7
		6.0	14.8	10.6	15.6	17.0	30.3		
30.9.80	4453.3	362.8	756.8	384.2	619.3	646.9	1683.3	11.7	17.0
		8.2	17.0	8.6	13.9	14.5	37.8		
30.9.81	4629.7	263.7	899.0	385.2	443.7	654.9	1983.2	13.0	18.4
		5.7	19.4	8.3	9.6	14.2	42.8		
30.9.82	4666.9	209.1	879.8	409.4	362.0	594.1	2212.5	14.5	18.8
		4.5	18.9	8.8	7.8	12.7	47.4		
30.9.83	4534.9	147.9	736.2	438.8	345.3	412.6	2453.9	17.2	21.3
		3.3	16.2	9.7	7.6	9.1	54.1		
30.9.84	4363.6	161.2	530.4	498.2	347.9	319.3	2506.5	18.9	23.2
		3.7	12.2	11.4	8.0	7.3	57.4		
31.12.85	4378.9	210.1	432.8	449.0	398.9	311.0	2577.2	19.8	25.2
		4.8	9.9	10.3	9.1	7.1	58.9		
31.12.86	4512.7	252.7	474.1	333.5	451.9	330.5	2670.0	19.9	26.1
		5.6	10.5	7.4	10.0	7.3	59.2		

Source: Statistisches Bundesamt, own calculations. Implied mean durations are calculated as the inverse of discrete time constant hazard rates, without and with correction for variations in gross influx, respectively. +About 6% not categorized.

Since significant guest worker influx had only a history of about 17 years in 1977, but a history of 26 years in 1986, the fraction of foreigners having stayed for a long period might be higher in 1986 even if the re-migration propensities of immigrants had not changed at all. To distinguish statistical from behavioral causes, I also estimated return propensities from the data at all ten data points taken separately, now taking into account the timing and magnitude of the gross influx of foreigners into Germany since 1960. These estimates strengthen the impression of a rising average completed duration of stay. However, these results should be interpreted with care. Data on gross influx is contaminated by grouping guest workers and applicants for political asylum into one category, and in calculating the size of the immigrant population I have abstracted from the difficulties created by repeated re-migration and re-entry and by births. Nevertheless, all the aspects raised here demonstrate that Germany has been an immigration country in the past.

Table 7: The Percentage of Foreigners to Population in Selected States and Cities in Germany, 1987

Hessen	9.7 %	Frankfurt/Main	24.5 %
Baden-Württemberg	9.5 %	Stuttgart	18.7 %
Nordrhein-Westfalen	8.4 %	Düsseldorf	17.0 %
Bayern	6.5 %	München	18.3 %
Hamburg	11.6 %	Berlin (West)	13.6 %

Source: Institut der deutschen Wirtschaft

Another similarity to the immigration experience of typical immigration countries lies in the pattern of location choice. Particularly in the United States, immigrants tend to concentrate in large cities. Table 7 demonstrates that this phenomenon can apparently also be observed in Germany. In this table, the percentages of foreigners in 4 German states are compared with the percentages of foreigners in their major cities. In each case, the urban percentage is at least double that of the entire state. In addition, one can see that the city-states of Hamburg and Berlin have higher percentages of foreigners than other states.

5 Concluding Remarks

The preceding sections have argued that an understanding of the labor market consequences of immigration has recently become an issue in Germany. Large numbers of permanent immigrants are expected from eastern and southern of Europe, as well as from the Third World. The most important considerations are the ability of immigrants to integrate into the German labor market and their potential burden on the welfare system. In addition, the earnings and employment prospects of native workers will be determined to a considerable extent by the substitutability of immigrant labor for native labor.

Most of the existing evidence on labor market effects of migration has been produced using United States data material. Although these results allow interesting speculations for Germany, the US labor market structure is very different, and hardly any results from these studies seem to carry over directly to the German case. Thus, the econometric techniques developed in this literature should be adapted to German data and to German institutional regulations. Since most of the immigrant influx to Germany had been guest workers and since Germany is not regarded as an immigration country in the public debate, one could claim, that this empirical work and the calculation of reliable forecasts of future developments based on existing German data material are impossible.

I have argued, in contrast, that Germany has already experienced large gross and net immigration, that guest workers have been integrated more and more into the German labor market, and that a large number of these guest workers should be viewed as permanent migrants. Thus, I have provided arguments for accepting Germany as the immigration country it has, in fact, been for years. As a consequence, empirical research can indeed utilize existing data material and government policy should use the insights created by this research to control the magnitude and the composition of the flow of immigration to Germany.

References

Altonji, Joseph and Card, David (1990): The Effects of Immigration on the Labor Market Outcomes of Natives; in: Freeman, Richard B. and Abowd, John M. (eds.); Immigration, Trade, and the Labor Market, Chicago: University of Chicago Press

Berry, R. Albert and Soligo, Ronald (1969): Some Welfare Aspects of International Migration; Journal of Political Economy, vol.77, pp.778-794

Borjas, George J. (1987): Self-Selection and the Earnings of Immigrants; American Economic Review, vol.77, pp.521-553

Borjas, George J. (1990): Friends or Strangers: The Impact of Immigrants on the U.S. Economy, New York: Basic Books

Butcher, Kristin F. and Card, David (1991): Immigration and Wages: Evidence from the 1980's; American Economic Review, vol.81, pp.292-296

Card, David (1990): The Impact of the Mariel Boatlift on the Miami Labor Market; Industrial and Labor Relations Review, vol.43, pp.245-257

Chiswick, Barry R. (1978): The Effects of Americanization on the Earnings of Foreign-Born Men; Journal of Political Economy, vol.86, pp.897-921

Dustmann, Christian (1993): Earnings Adjustments of Temporary Migrants; Journal of Population Economics, vol. 6, pp. 153-168

Franz, Wolfgang (1991): International Migratory Movements: The German Experience; University of Konstanz Disc. Paper Serie II No. 160

Harris, John R. and Todaro, Michael P. (1970): Migration, Unemployment and Development: A Two-Sector Analysis; American Economic Review, vol.60, pp.126-142

Institut der deutschen Wirtschaft (1990): Zahlen zur wirtschaftlichen Entwicklung der Bundesrepublik Deutschland, Köln: Deutscher Instituts-Verlag

Licht, Georg and Steiner, Viktor (1993): Assimilation, Labour Market Experience, and Earnings Profiles of Temporary and Permanent Immigrant Workers in Germany; ZEW Discussion Paper No.93-06

McCall, Brian P. and McCall, John J. (1987): A Sequential Study of Migration and Job Search; Journal of Labor Economics, vol.5, pp.452-476

Pischke, Jörn-Steffen (1992): Assimilation and the Earnings of Guestworkers in Germany; ZEW Discussion Paper No.92-17

Roy, Andrew D. (1951): Some Thoughts on the Distribution of Earnings; Oxford Economic Papers, vol.3, pp.80-93

Schmidt, Christoph M. (1992a): Country-of-Origin Differences in the Earnings of German Immigrants; University of Munich Discussion Paper No.92-29

Schmidt, Christoph M. (1992b): The Earnings Dynamics of Immigrant Labor; University of Munich Discussion Paper No.29-28

Schmidt, Christoph M. and Zimmermann, Klaus F. (1992): Migration Pressure in Germany: Past and Future; in: Zimmermann, Klaus F. (ed.): Migration and Economic Development, Berlin et al.: Springer, pp.201-230

Statistisches Bundesamt (1970 - 1991): <u>Statistische Jahrbücher für die Bundesrepublik Deutschland. Statistische Jahrbücher für das Ausland</u>, Wiesbaden

Straubhaar, Thomas and Zimmermann, Klaus F. (1992): <u>Towards a European Migration Policy</u>; CEPR Discussion Paper No.641

The Future Growth of Foreign Population in Germany[1]

Ralf E. Ulrich
Faculty of Social Sciences
Humboldt University Berlin
Unter den Linden 6
10099 Berlin, Germany

1 Introduction

Immigration to Germany has increased to unprecedented levels in the past few years. Recent population projections deal with a wide range of immigration assumptions for the next decades. But they avoid to make explicit what the continuation of the current level would imply for the structure of population in Germany. Up to now only a very small minority of foreigners become naturalized under the *ius sanguinis*. This makes Germany's share of foreign population look higher than in most other European countries. The future course of immigration will be influenced by its impact on national interest and wealth, by humanitarian considerations and by the ability of German institutions to regulate immigration. This paper cannot predict any of these factors. Instead, it tries to illustrate the demographic consequences of basic scenarios with regard to the share of foreigners within the population, their age composition, settlement structure, etc. Past immigration and the contribution of foreigners' birth surplus are dicussed to get an analytical background.

A first section gives an overview of recent projections for the population of Germany in total. Most of the projections deal with immigration but none gives a long-term figure for the absolute number and share of foreigners. A second section gives the analytical background for past immigration to Germany. A third section does the same for past development of foreigners' fertility. The assumptions for the projections are discussed in section four. The results are finally presented in section five.

---

[1] This paper is based on research supported by the German Research Foundation (DFG).

2 Recent Population Projections for Germany

With the reunification Germany became larger in population than any other state in Europe, except for the former Soviet Union. The former Federal Republic of Germany and the German Democratic Republic kept many similarities in culture through-out the forty years of artifical division. On the other hand differences emerged not only in the political and economic sphere, but also with regard to population development. After 1989 East Germany lost more than a million inhabitants to West Germany through migration. Other dynamic changes in the field of population are taking place in the united Germany. In the East births have decreased to half the level of 1989. Annual immigration reached unprecedented levels in the past few years. These dynamic developments have induced an increased interest in the demographic future of Germany.

Several population projections have been published recently. Table 1 shows the results of five projections.

Table 1: Recent Population Projections for Germany, in Mio.

	2000	2010	2020	2030	2040
1992 Official Projection	81.1	78.9	74.9	69.9	
DIW					
moderate immigr.	83.4	83.7	81.6		73.4
high immigr.	85.4	85.9	84.4		77.5
H. Birg, Bielefeld					
with immigr.	81.5	80.9	79.1	76.1	
without immigr.	78.3	74.7	69.7	63.5	
BfLR					
moderate immigr.	83.0		79.0		
UN Popul. projections 1992					
low variant	81.0	79.8	75.5		
medium variant	82.5	84.1	84.3		
high variant	84.4	88.9	92.2		

Sources: see text

The German Statistical Office published its first official population forecast for the united Germany (*7. koordinierte Bevölkerungsvorausschätzung*) in early 1992 (Sommer, 1992). With regard to fertility development a continuation of current levels is assumed for West Germany. This means a total fertility rate (TFR) of 1.4, as in 1989, is supposed to prevail until 2030. For East Germany a recovery of fertility is expected to take place after the steep decline: the TFR should gradually approach the West German level until 1995 and then remain constant.

Where mortality is concerned a gain of two years life expectancy is assumed for the West and an approach of East German life expectancy until 2030.

Concerning immigration the authors from the Statistical Office supposed a sharp decline. Like other authors they expected the immigration of ethnic Germans from Eastern Europe (*Aussiedler*) to decline until zero in the year 2000 (See also: Schulz, 1990). With regard to the net immigration of foreigners the projections assumed a decline to an annual average of 60 thousand in the first decade of the next century. Later the net immigration would decline further to an annual average of 53 thousand. The authors justified these figures with the expectation of a more restricted use of immigration regulations in Germany and/or a decrease of emigration pressure in Eastern Europe.

The projections of Erika Schulz from the German Institute for Economic Research (*Deutsches Institut für Wirtschaftsforschung, DIW*) differ mainly because of the immigration assumptions.(Schulz, 1993). Her fertility scenario is very close to the assumptions of the Statistical Office. Her lower immigration scenario expects 550.000 immigrants for 1993, around 375.000 for the following two years and 280.000 per annum until 2000. From 2001 to 2010 annual immigration would continue with 190.000. Her high scenario assumes 430.000 annual immigrants from 1996 to 2000 and 260.000 immigrants in each year from 2001 to 2010. Clearly Erika Schulz expects a very different world with regard to future immigration. But even the high immigration scenario leads to a decline of population in her calculations until 2040.

Birg and Flöthmann (University of Bielefeld) use an approach based on cohort analysis to fix the fertility assumptions for their projections (Birg/Flöthmann, 1993). They expect a TFR close to 1.4 in West Germany until 2010 and a slow recovery of fertility in East Germany, reaching TFR 1.0 in 2000 and 1.3 in 2010. Immigration is expected to decrease to 254.000 in 1995 and to remain constant later.

The Federal Research Institute for Regional Geography and Planning (*Bundesanstalt für Landeskunde und Raumordnung, BfLR*) has published a population projection for Germany, disaggregated to 97 regions (BfLR, 1993). The main results are given only until 2000. The BfLR assumed a TFR of 1.36 for West Germany until 2000 and an increase of East German TFR to 1.0 in 2000. The immigration balance is expected to decrease from 500.000 in 1993 to 350.000 in 1996 and to remain at this level later.

The highest available population projections for Germany are made by the UN Population Division in its 1992 assessment. Only in the low scenario they assume fertility levels as commonly extrapolated within Germany. The medium scenario expects the TFR to increase to 1.8 in 2010, the high scenario assumes an increase to 2.1.

This little overview has shown that population projections for Germany assume at least in part a continuation of the high immigration rates of the past few years for a longer period. One might argue that this is an extrapolation of a short time experience. On the other hand this extrapolation could be justified with the new geopolitical situation of Germany after the fall of the iron curtain or with a new age of international migration. Another argument for high immigration is the need to compensate the aging of the German population. The level of future immigration to Germany will not be totally independent of its effects, even if attempts for a regulation are limited in their efficiency. Only if the integration of immigrants succeeds a long term continuation on a high level is probable. But how much would the share of foreigners grow under different immigration scenarios? And how are the prospects for a successful integration? In any case it makes sense to look a few more years back and analyse the growth of foreign population in the past 30 years.

3 The Past Growth of Germany's Foreign Population

Immigration played a major role in the population development of West Germany after World War II. From 1944 to 1946 about 6 million German expellees (*Vertriebene*) came from Eastern Europe to the territory of the later Federal Republic, another 2 million expellees came until 1950. Their economic integration was very difficult in the first years. In the fifties the German "economic miracle" began and unemployment decreased rapidly. The German immigrants from Eastern Europe could be integrated almost completely into the labour market.

Another important source of immigration to West Germany in the post-war period were resettlers from East Germany (*Übersiedler*). More than 3.5 million people came between 1950 and 1961 (Bethlehem, 1982, p. 26). The push factors on the side of the German Democratic Republic were of political as well as of economic nature. With the erection of the Berlin Wall in 1961 this source of immigration to West Germany was closed.

For the accelerated economic growth in West Germany sufficient and cheap labour supply was essential. This was already felt in the fifties, when structural misfits led to labor shortages in a situation of still moderate unemployment. While in 1955 there were more than 1 million unemployed in West Germany, 25 percent of the enterprises expected labor shortages. In 1959 still more than half of the enterprises had these kind of worries (Thränhardt, 1992, p. 170ff). First attempts to recruit temporary labor migrants (guest workers, *Gastarbeiter*) were already made in the fifties. A first agreement on the recruitment of workers was concluded with Italy in 1955, agreements with Spain and Greece followed in 1960. Other agreements were concluded with Turkey, Portugal, Morocco, Tunesia and Spain. The migration treaties emphasized the temporary nature of labor migration as being in the interest of the countries of origin, the migrants and Germany.

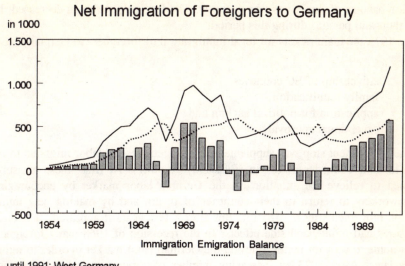

until 1991: West Germany
Data: Statistisches Bundesamt

Chart 1

Chart 1 shows the annual immigration and emigration of foreigners to Germany. The high level of immigration but also of emigration indicates a substantial turnover in the foreign population. 20 million foreigners immigrated to Germany in 1954 to 1992, while 14.3 million foreigners emigrated in the same period. The net migration balance was 5.7 million. Over the whole period there were on average 366 thousand foreigners emigrating annually. It is important to note that until the mid eighties there were several periods with a negative migration balance for foreigners.

The main pull factor for guestworker immigration was the economic strength of West Germany and its wage level in particular. Since immigration was closely related to economic pull factors it reacted to the recession in the second half of the sixties. While emigration remained at almost the same level from 1966 to 1967, immigration reacted very sensitivly to the German recession. It decreased to almost half the level of 1966. The recession was very short and net immigration increased again to values of more than 500 thousand per year in 1969 and 1970.

In October 1973 the German government stopped the official recruitment of guestworkers (*Anwerbestopp*), reacting to an overheated economy and infrastructural bottlenecks. Similar measures had been taken by Switzerland (1970), Sweden (1972) and France (1974), as well as by other countries. The oil price shock in late 1973 and the following recession with high and persistent unemployment changed the need for immigrant labor in Germany. These factors had a steep influence on net immigration in the short run. In the years 1974 to 1977 the migration balance of foreigners was negative. The foreign population decreased by 430 thousand persons during this period.

Since 1973 the main tickets for legal immigration of foreigners to Germany have been:

- citizenship of EC countries,
- family reunification,
- application for political asylum and
- exceptional approval.

The recruitment stop was supplemented by incentives for labor migrants to return to their countries of origin (*Rückkehrförderung*). At first these measures seemed to relieve the situation on the German labor market by encouraging guestworkers to return to their countries of origin and by making new immigration movements more difficult. But after a few years it appeared that these measures had unintended side effects. In the recession of 1968 many foreigners went home to wait for better times on the German labor market in order to return there later. After 1973 an increasing number of foreigners realized that they would like to stay permanently in Germany. While unsure about Germany's future policy concerning labor migration they preferred to stay in Germany even when unemployed. An important increase of emigration took place only in 1974. Beginning in 1976 the emigration of foreigners started decreasing. Simultaneously labor migrants brought their families to Germany, making immigration increase again after 1976. Within the next four years the foreign population in Germany again had a positive migration balance, more than compensating the loss of 1974 to 1977.

The recession of 1981/82 again brought the migration balance of foreigners into the negative range for three years. Immigration decreased in 1981 by 20 percent and in 1982 again by 36 percent. Emigration did not react that sensitively. Net emigration reached almost 213 thousand in 1984.

At the end of the eighties net immigration of foreigners increased again to levels observed in the early seventies. In 1988 the foreign population in Germany grew by almost 290 thousand persons, due to migration. In the following years net immigration increased continuously to the highest level ever recorded: 593 thousand in 1992. Together with ethnic German immigrants (*Aussiedler, Übersiedler*) Germany reached a migration surplus of 977 thousand in 1989 and even more than 1 million in 1990. This came close to the annual level of permanent immigration into the United States at that time. But the US has about three times the population of Germany.

Until 1992 the rapid increase of immigration was accompanied by a favorable economic situation. West Germany experienced its greatest increase of employment in the past 30 years. An important reason for the boom was the gain of the East German market. The huge public transfers from West to East Germany had the effect of an "export" promotion program for the West German industry. But the positive employment effect of this situation could not persist very long. It was accompanied by a massive employment crisis in the East and financed mainly by deficit spending. The employment expansion came to a halt in 1992. Since then unemployment has been increasing in West Germany. For 1993 a GDP decrease between 1.5 and 2 percent is expected for the united Germany.

It is not only the dimension of immigration that has changed recently, but also its composition and character. Until 1980 asylum seekers were a slowly growing but less important segment of immigrants. This changed in 1980, when applicants for political asylum made up 17 percent of all immigrating foreigners. After 1990 the absolute number of asylum seekers increased sharply, reaching 438 thousand in 1992 (see table 2).

While applying for political asylum at Germany' borders the applicants enter a lengthy legal procedure to decide if they fulfil the German legal definition of political refugees. Until 1993 Germany did not ratify the Dublin agreement allowing potential applicants for asylum to apply only in the first EC country they enter. Actually only a small share of applicants successfully receives political asylum when their application has been legally decided. Only 4.4 percent of persons applying in 1990 for political asylum were finally recognized for this status. But only another minority of the non-accepted applicants were deported: 6.5 percent. About 18 percent of the applicants from 1990 went back home voluntarily. The rest remained in Germany because of humanitarian, legal or other reasons.

Germany's geographic position, its specific regulations for political asylum and the universal entitlement of applicants for social security benefits made the country a popular destination for potential applicants. In 1992 62 percent of all asylum seekers in the EC countries came to Germany. The number of past asylum seekers cumulated here to more than 1.5 million refugees among the foreign population at the end of 1992. Among them were:

- persons entitled to political asylum
- relatives of the first group
- refugees in special contingents (among others boat people from Vietnam)
- homeless foreigners
- de-facto refugees (asylum legally refused, but not deported)
- applicants for political asylum, waiting for a decision

The specific situation of asylum seekers made an integration very difficult. With July 1991 work permits were given to asylum applicants, waiting for a decision about their status. But entrance in to the labor market is very difficult, since most of the asylum seekers don't speak German.

Table 2: The growing importance of asylum seekers

	Immigration (1)	Net immigration (2)	Asylum seekers (3)	(3)/(1), %
1970	976232	541580	8645	0,9
1971	870737	370479	5388	0,6
1972	787162	272716	5289	0,7
1973	869109	342298	5595	0,6
1974	542425	-39535	9424	1,7
1975	367318	-233053	9627	2,6
1976	388158	-127446	11123	2,9
1977	423499	-28734	16410	3,9
1978	456724	50728	33136	7,3
1979	545918	179765	51493	9,4
1980	632285	246250	107818	17,1
1981	501960	86210	49391	9,8
1982	322449	-111449	37423	11,6
1983	276448	-148741	19737	7,1
1984	333297	-213160	35278	10,6
1985	399951	32232	73832	18,5
1986	479518	131528	99650	20,8
1987	473341	139137	57379	12,1
1988	648550	289461	103076	15,9
1989	770771	332494	121318	15,7
1990	842364	376326	193063	22,9
1991	920491	423015	256112	27,8
1992	1207602	592855	438191	36,3

Data: Statistisches Bundesamt

For 1992 the Ministry of the Interior announced that 450.000 asylum seekers had been supported by public means. The estimated annual cost of 15.500 DM per capita consisted of 8.500 DM for social security benefits and 7.000 DM for dormitories and infrastructure. The total expenses for refugees have been estimated by the German government at 8 billion DM. This is about 20 percent of the budget for social security benefits (*Sozialhilfe*).

The discrepancy between the rapidly rising number of asylum seekers and the small share fulfilling the legal conditions gave way for a growing scepticism about the abuse of asylum as an immigration ticket. For a large part of German society it was clear that the high level of immigrants applying for political asylum in 1992 could not be maintained in the next years. In the first half of 1993 a change in the basic law concerning the right for political asylum was passed.

Since July 1 asylum seekers can be deported if they come from "safe" countries of origin or if they enter Germany through a "safe" transit country. Since all German neighbor countries are regarded as "safe", asylum seekers can enter only by airplane or ship. In 1992 75 percent of all applicants came by land, mostly from Tschechia or Poland. It is too early now to evaluate the effect of the new asylum regulation. In July the number of asylum applications dropped by one third.

The growth of the number of asylum seekers was obviously independent of the economic situation and the absorption capacity of the labor market. This is an important feature of this segment of immigration. It has continuously delinked the immigration process of the last few years from economic conditions in the host country. It will depend on political institutions to re-establish this link again.

Since foreigners are defined by citizenship, *naturalization* might potentially be a factor reducing their number. The legal basis for this is still a law from 1913 (*Reichs- und Staatsangehörigkeitsgesetz*). German citizenship follows the ius sanguinis. Children born in marriage receive German citizenship if one parent is German. Extra-marital children are German if the mother is. Naturalization is relatively easy if foreigners marry a German partner. Foreigners can apply for citizenship after 10 years of living in Germany. This applies to more than 60 percent of the foreign population. There are several other requirements for naturalization, like not relying on social security or unemployment benefits and having a permanent residence. Until June 1993 there was an administrative fee of 5000 DM for naturalization, now it is 500 DM. For foreigners of the second generation the foreigners law of 1977 (*Ausländergesetz*) allows a simplified naturalization (*erleichterte Einbürgerung*) if they apply between the ages of 16 and 23, have been living for more than 8 years, have not been convicted of any crime and give up their previous citizenship. The last condition seems to be the main obstacle for naturalization. The claim for simplified naturalization by young foreigners is still rather low. But in a representative inquiry 72 percent of the Ex-Yugoslavian and 60 percent of the Turkish teenagers declared that they would like to be naturalized if they could keep their previous citizenship. But still double-citizenship is only allowed as an exception.

The number of naturalizations of foreigners[2] has been rather low in the past. From the seventies to the end of the eighties it was been always close to 13.000 or 14.000 cases per year, with remarkably low fluctuations. Beginning in 1988 the number of naturalizations increased to reach 27.295 cases in 1991. The annual rate of naturalizations was between 0.3 percent and 0.5 percent (1991) of the foreign population. The low rate of naturalization has to be kept in mind when comparing the share of the foreign population with other countries. With about 8 percent in 1992 Germany is among the European countries with the

---

[2] This refers to naturalization of non-Germans (*Ermessenseinbürgerung*). The formal naturalization of ethnic German resettlers (*Anspruchseinbürgerung*) has always been 3 to 4 times higher.

highest share of foreign population. But if Swedish or French naturalization laws were applied in Germany, the foreign population would be about 30 percent of its present size.

In the past 30 years the foreign population was grew not only because of a positive immigration balance. The *birth surplus* has substantially contributed to its growth. Germans and foreigners are separately listed in the German birth and death statistics after 1960. From that time until 1988 foreigners had a cumulated birth surplus of 1.6 million. Compared with an immigration surplus of 3.9 million natural growth contributed about 29 percent to the total growth of the foreign population.[3] The future contribution of natural growth will depend on the fertility development of foreigners.

4 The Development of Foreigner's Fertility

With the beginning of guest worker immigration in the sixties the number of foreign births in Germany was initially below 20 thousand per year. At that time it were mainly young single men who came from Southern Europe to Germany. With the increasing share of immigrating women and a tendency to stay longer in Germany the number of births increased to a peak of more than 100 thousand in 1974 (see table 3).

After 1974 the number of foreign births declined until 1985. This is partly due to a change in the legal status of children in mixed marriages. Until 1974 legitimate children with a foreign father and illegitimate children with a foreign mother were understood as being foreigners. After 1975 only legitimate children with both parents being foreigners were registered as foreigners. The status of illegitimate children remained as before. For the birth register children with a foreign father and a German mother were then Germans while they had been counted as foreigners before. This applied than to more 10 percent of the foreign births in 1974.

The number of foreign births continued to decline after 1975 until it reached a minimum of 53 thousand in 1985. It is obvious that this was no longer the reflection of a change in registration but a genuine fertility decline. But the dimensions of this decline are difficult to determine. While the number of foreign births is registered in Germany fairly accurately, the number of foreign women in each age group is only roughly estimated by the Statistical Office. The number of foreigners updated from birth and death registration and migration sta-

---

[3] While Germans had a birth surplus of 2.95 million from 1960 to 1972, they had a death surplus of nearly the same dimension in the following period. Thus, the foreigner´s birth surplus made up 70 percent of the natural growth of the population in Germany from 1960 to 1988.

tistics showed a severe difference of 566 thousand persons to the census result in 1987. Therefore the calculation of a total fertility rate for foreigners and any following assessment of foreigner's fertility decline is flawed by the inaccuracy of estimates concerning the potential number of mothers.

Table 3: Births and deaths, 1960-88

	Births		Deaths	
	Germans	foreigners	Germans	foreigners
1960	957.488	11.141	639.369	3.593
1961	998.732	13.955	623.531	4.030
1962	999.749	18.803	640.558	4.261
1963	1.029.448	24.675	668.277	4.792
1964	1.034.580	30.857	638.903	5.225
1965	1.006.470	37.858	672.093	5.535
1966	1.005.199	45.146	680.499	5.822
1967	972.027	47.432	681.721	5.628
1968	924.877	44.948	728.172	5.876
1969	852.783	50.673	737.407	6.953
1970	747.804	63.004	726.838	8.005
1971	697.812	80.714	721.605	9.065
1972	609.773	91.441	721.673	9.591
1973	536.547	99.086	721.393	9.635
1974	518.103	108.270	718.234	9.277
1975	504.639	95.873	740.269	8.991
1976	515.898	86.953	724.577	8.563
1977	504.073	78.271	696.885	8.037
1978	501.475	74.993	715.174	8.044
1979	506.424	75.560	703.642	8.090
1980	539.962	80.695	705.606	8.511
1981	544.548	80.009	713.663	8.529
1982	548.192	72.981	707.333	8.524
1983	532.706	61.471	710.273	8.064
1984	529.362	54.795	688.283	7.835
1985	532.405	53.750	696.602	7.694
1986	567.310	58.653	694.045	7.845
1987	574.819	67.191	679.389	8.030
1988	603.741	73.518	678.918	8.598
1989	601.669	79.868		
1990	640.879	86.320		

Source: Statistisches Bundesamt

Proebsting (1988, p. 84) gives estimates of the total fertility rate for Germans and foreigners. According to his calculations foreigners had a TFR of 2.6 in

1977, as opposed to Germans with 1.3. Until 1985 the foreigners' TFR declined to 1.67 and increased slightly to 1.76 in the following year.

Table 4: Total Fertility Rate: Germans and foreigners

	Germans	Foreigners
1975	1,34	2,64
1976	1,36	2,57
1977	1,32	2,40
1978	1,30	2,33
1979	1,30	2,32
1980	1,37	2,38
1981	1,36	2,28
1982	1,35	2,08
1983	1,29	1,82
1984	1,26	1,69
1985	1,25	1,67
1986	1,31	1,76

Source: Proebsting, 1988

The fertility of foreigners adjusted not only in level but also in the age structure to German fertility. Fertility concentrated most at the age between 20 and 30. Adolescent fertility and fertility over 30 decreased not only absolutely but also in the share of all births. While there were 257 births by mothers between ages 15-19 in 1970 there were only 194 births by mothers in this age group in 1987. 723 foreign babies were born in 1970 by mothers above the age of 30, while only 504 such babies where born in 1987.

There are substantial differences between the main nationalities with regard to fertility. The highest fertility have Turkish mothers, while Spanish and Greek mothers had total fertility rates below those of German mothers even at the end of the eighties (see chart 2). These differences suggest that changes of the average fertility of foreigners might well depend on the composition with regard to nationalities. That might explain slight increases like the one in 1986.

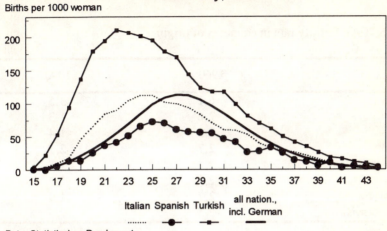

Chart 2

The fertility decline of foreigners in Germany could be explained along three lines. First, it reflects recent changes in reproductive behavior in the countries of origin. In most of the countries of origin there has been a fertility decline in the past decades (see table 5). After the strong fertility decline in Germany there was a substantial gap to fertility levels in the countries of origin at the beginning of the seventies. But in the past twenty years fertility has fallen below replacement level in all of the main countries of origin. One exception is Turkey with a total fertility rate of more than 3.5 in 1990. But in relative terms the fertility decline in Turkey was even faster than in the other countries. It should be expected that the foreigners in Germany are also influenced by the change in values and attitudes taking place in their native country.

Secondly, the reproductive behavior of foreigners is gradually adjusting to German values. This effect should be stronger if there is a real social and cultural integration. It is supposed to be most effective in intermarriages. But even in a continued cultural segregation there are several potential channels of influence, like mass media, consumption patterns, etc. It has to be noted that the fertility level of foreign nationalities was substantially lower in the eighties than in the respective countries of origin. The TFR for Turkish women in Germany was 2.9 in 1987 while in Turkey it was well above 3. Spanish women in Germany had a TFR of 0.9 in the same year.

Thirdly, the development of foreigners' fertility is influenced by their specific situation as newcomers trying to make their fortune in another country. For a long time the labor force participation rate (LFPR) of foreign women in Germany was much higher than of native women. In 1974 the LFPR for foreign women was 46 percent, while German women had an LFPR of 30 percent. In the following years the LFPR of foreign women has leveled off with the German female LFPR. In 1988 both groups had the same LFPR of 37 percent.

Table 5: Total fertility rate in countries of origin

Country	1960	1990
Turkey	6,1	3,5
Italy	2,6	1,3
Spain	2,9	1,4
Poland	2,7	2,1
Portugal	3,1	1,5
Greece	2,2	1,5
Yugoslavia	2,7	1,9
memo: Germany	2,5	*1,5*

Data: UN Population Division, 1992 assessment

Two conclusions can be drawn from the discussion of fertility adjustment. First: the level and structure of future immigration will influence the fertility of foreigners. If there had been no strong immigration of Turks in the seventies, the fertility of foreigners in Germany would already have been much lower today. But the differences in fertility within Europe are lower than in the past. Only if a substantial share of future immigrants comes from high-fertility countries of the Third World an important impact can be expected. Otherwise the impact of level and structure of immigration on fertility will be moderate. Secondly, it can be expected that the birth surplus of foreigners will decrease. Therefore the foreign population in Germany will experience a similar aging process as the German population.

5 Assumptions for the Projections

The main factor determining the future size of the foreign population will be *immigration*. Inevitable, assumptions in this field are to a certain extent arbitrary, especially when it comes to concrete figures. In a less specific view two basic scenarios for the future course of immigration can be imagined.

One scenario is the continuation of Germany's experiences with immigration in the past 30 years until 1989. This scenario would imply that the high level of immigration in the last few years was a unique phenomenon and that it will not continue for a long time. Obviously the pressure for immigration to Germany has increased with the fall of the iron curtain and the transformation crisis in Eastern Europe and with the war in Ex-Yugoslavia, to name only two important factors. Germany was not prepared to react to this situation with a regulation of immigration according to its national interest. The case of asylum has shown how difficult such a reaction was for its political institutions. Other topics in the context of immigration and the integration of immigrants are still not answered by an institutional reaction.

After the unification, Germany's internal situation has changed with regard to the need of immigration. In 1989 there was an unsatisfied labor demand in West Germany. But the adjustment crisis in the East German economy has led to open unemployment and underemployment in the East, thus reaching levels equal to those during the Great Depression. One million East Germans have moved to the West after 1989, 500.000 commute to the West for work. They are competitors for foreigners on the West German labor market. The unemployment rate of foreigners in Germany is two times higher than the general rate. Recent analyses show that there are only few branches with a potential for further employment expansion in the next years. This labor demand could easily be satisfied by reducing current levels of unemployment and underemployment.

Following this perspective one could expect that Germany's institutions will react to the increased immigration pressure and the limited need for immigration with further attempts to regulate immigration. A comprehensive policy in this field would include efforts to support the integration of past immigrants. Following the experience of other countries one should expect the efficiency of these efforts to be limited.

One basic idea of the first scenario is that the labor market need for future immigration is not larger than in the past 30 years. Actually there are arguments that it might be even lower. The second element of this scenario is that after a period of adjustment German institutions will succeed to limit immigration to a level defined by national interests. For the illustrative projections in this paper it is necessary to bring these hypotheses down to concrete figures. We would then assume annual net immigration to decrease to 250 thousand in 1995. It would continue to decrease to 60 thousand in the year 2000 (the average of net immigration in the past 15 years before 1990) and remain on that level.

A second immigration scenario should consider a higher level of immigration. It could become reality if a higher level of immigration is intended to compensate the aging of the German population. But it could also materialize if institutions fail to regulate immigration. In this case the experience of the past few years could give an orientation. To illustrate this case only a slight reduction to 400.000 annual net immigration in 1995 has been assumed. Immigration was then assumed to remain constant on this level.

As already discussed in the analytical section *fertility* has a less intense effect on the growth of the foreign population and it depends in turn of the level of immigration. For the first scenario it was assumed that the total fertility rate of foreigners will decrease to 1.5 in 2000 and remain constant here-after. In case of a much higher level of immigration (second scenario) the total fertiltiy rate was assumed to reach 1.6 in 2000 and to stay on that level.

Mortality has a small range of potential scenarios and only a minor influence. There are no life tables available for the foreign population in Germany. According to the official death registration there are on annual average only 8 thousand deaths by foreigners. This translates to a crude death rate of 1.8 per 1000. From sociological research we know that in the past some guestworkers preferred to spend the last years of their life in their native countries. On the other hand an increasing number of foreigners brought their parents to Germany after sucessfully establishing themselves here. Data on the age structure of international migration show emigration and immigration movements at the age of 65 and older at nearly the same level. In 1989 the immigration of foreigners in this age group was by 3 thousand higher than the emigration. So, the low death rate has to be attributed to the juvenile age structure of the foreign population.

As with fertility there is also an adjustment of mortality to German levels to be expected. The differences between life expectancy in Germany and in the countries of origin have been reduced in the past twenty years. With regard to adult foreigners one should not expect a too high gain in life expectancy while in Germany. Since many guestworkers are employed in jobs with high exposure to health risks there might even be negative factors. On the other hand the infant and child mortality of foreigners in Germany is much lower than in the countries of origin. Foreigners' infant mortality has been reduced from 23.1 per 1000 in 1970 to 8.8 per 1000 in 1988. One should expect the level of mortality for foreigners somewhere between the situation in their countries of origin and the German level of life expectancy.

For the mortality assumption an average of life expectancy at birth in the main countries of origin has been calculated. As a weight the share of each nationality in all foreigners has been used. This average life expectancy was 67.7 for men and 72.4 for women in 1990. Life expectancy in West Germany was 72.6 for men and 79 for women then. When using the weighted average procedure for infant mortality in the countries of origin an infant mortality of 38 per 1000 was calculated for 1990. This is much higher than the 8.8 for foreigners in Germany.

Only one mortality assumption has been used for both scenarios. To consider the effect of improved infant mortality on life expectancy, values of 70 for males and 76 for females have been taken as the starting point for the mortality assumptions. For the future development of mortality an increase of foreigners' life expectancy by 2.5 years in twenty years has been assumed.

A reference scenario has been computed for the German population. It assumed a constant total fertility rate of 1.4 and a gain of life expectancy by 3 years until 2010. The immigration of ethnic Germans from Eastern Europe (*Aussiedler*) was assumed to decrease to 150.000 in 1995 and to remain on that level until 2005. This implies the complete resettlement of the *Aussiedler* population from Eastern Europe over the next 12 years.

6 Results and Main Implications

The German population will decrease under the given assumptions by more than 10 million within the next 40 years. This is quite in accordance with other projections as discussed in section 1.

Table 6 shows on overview of the results. If the immigration and naturalization regime of the past 20 years continued, as assumed in scenario 1, the number of foreigners would increase to 11.8 million in 2030. The share of foreign population in Germany would be then 15.7 percent, nearly double today's value. Germanys total population would be 75.3 million.

Table 6: Results of illustrative projections

		2010	2030
Foreign Population, Mio.	Scenario 1	10,2	11,8
	Scenario 2	16,0	27,1
Foreigners Pop. Share, %	Scenario 1	12,4	15,7
	Scenario 2	18,2	29,9
Age dependency rate, Foreigner	Scenario 1	0,218	0,492
	Scenario 2	0,152	0,262
Age dependency rate, total population	Scenario 1		0,720
	Scenario 2		0,590

Data: own calculations

Scenario 2 assumed levels of immigration like in the past few years (400,000 per year) to continue over a long period. In this case the total population in Germany would grow to 90.5 million in 2030. It would consist of 27 million foreigners and 63.5 million Germans. 30 percent of the population in Germany would be foreigners, if the definition of citizenship and the naturalization rate were "constant".

In the past the settlement of immigrating foreigners had a specific *regional pattern*, with obvious preferences for certain cities. The share of foreigners within the population in Frankfurt/Main or Offenbach is already above 20 percent. If the settlement preferences and regional concentration of foreigners were to persist, their share in these cities and regions would grow above average. In scenario 2 Frankfurt/Main would have a share of foreign population of about 64 percent in 2030. Foreigners would also be a majority in Offenbach, Munich, Stuttgart, Mannheim, Düsseldorf, Cologne and Duisburg. Even under the low immigration scenario the share of foreigners within the population in Frankfurt/Main would be 44 percent in 2030.

These figures seem to be unrealistic at first sight. But the result of the extrapolation suggests that a continuation of current levels of immigration with current naturalization policy would lead to a situation in which the majority of citizens in some German cities would have no right to vote.

No projections would be necessary only to illustrate the long-term effect of certain levels of immigration on the size of population. But projections als allow to draw conclusions about the future age structure. Chart 3 shows the corresponding age pyramids. The low share of older age groups will not remain even under the high growth scenario 2. The low share of older people is a unique phenomenon in the early build-up of an immigrant population. The age dependency rate of foreigners was 0.076 in 1990. Even under high immigration it would increase to 0.262 in 2030. With only 60,000 annual immigration after 2000 it would be 0.492 in 2030. What seems to make a great difference with regard to absolute numbers and share of foreigners makes only on little difference for the age dependency of the total population.

Age Structure of Foreigners

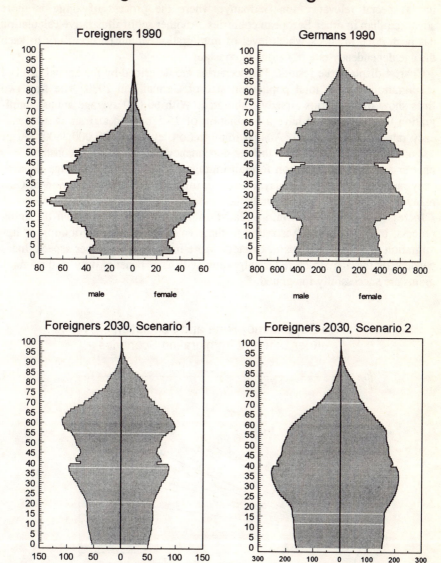

Data: 1990 Statistisches Bundesamt
2030 Projektions

Chart 3

The positive impact of immigration is still often used as an argument for higher levels of immigration or against any attempts to regulate its level. This argument has a special relevance for Germany, where the process of aging is more advanced than in other European countries. Another set of illustrative calculation has been done to check which level of immigration would be necessary to keep the age dependency rate in Germany constant.

Chart 4 displays the results. The scenarios are described by the annual level of immigration and the total population size of Germany in 2030. The first two lines show the scenarios already elaborated. With 60,000 average annual immigration Germany would have a population of 75.5 million and an age dependency rate of 0.73 in 2030. Annual immigration levels of 400,000, 800,000 or 1.2 million would fail to keep the age dependency rate in Germany constant. It is only at the level of 2 million foreign immigrants per year that the age dependency rate would remain at today's level. In this case the total population of Germany would be 165.7 million in 2030.

Increased immigration within a realistic range can only slow down the aging process, but not stop it. According to these calculation, the contribution of immigration is again lower than expected. More important is another aspect. Independent of the age structure, immigration will have benefits only if the immigrants are successfully integrated.

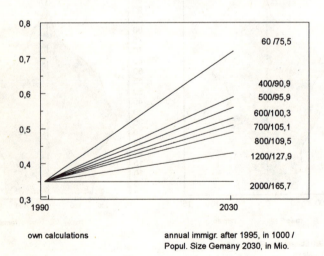

Chart 4

7 Conclusions

The aim of this paper was not to predict the future, but rather show the effects of different paths which are currently considered as possible. The long - term average of net immigration over the past decades seems to be low compared with the experience of the past few years. In any case, if immigration were to continue on this level the foreign population would grow close to double its current number until 2030. If the past few years were the model for a new era of immigration, as some authors believe, foreigners would reach a share of 30 percent of Germany's population within the next forty years. If the regional concentration of settlement of foreigners were as in the past, their population share in cities like Frankfurt/Main would be about 60 percent.

Immigration is sometimes seen as a compensation for the aging of population. These calculations show that even high levels of immigration cannot provide this. There are only gradual improvements of the age dependency rate. Since foreigners' fertility has already adjusted to German levels, the aging of the foreign population is more or less inevitable. The illustrative calculations of this paper underline that a long-term continuation of recent levels of immigration would imply a very different Germany. It is not sure if the country will be able to regulate future immigration according to its national interest. In any case its institutions and people will have to adjust to a very different situation within a comparably short period.

References

BfLR: Perspektiven der künftigen Bevölkerungsentwicklung in Deutschland. Informationen zur Raumentwicklung, Heft 9/10, 11/12 1993

Birg, H.: Demographische Wirkungen politischen Handelns. Eine deutsche Perspektive. In: H.-U. Klose (Hrsg): Die erfahrene Gesellschaft. Alternde Bevölkerung - dynamische Wirtschaft. Opladen 1993

Birg, H. unter Mitarbeit von E-J- Flöthmann; R. Tautz: Analyse und Prognose der Zahl der Lebendgeborenen in den alten und neuen Bundesländern bis zum Jahr 2000. Arbeitspapier des IBS, Institut für Bevölkerungsforschungund Sozialpolitik der Universität Bielefled, Bielefeld 1993

Birg, H.; E-J- Flöthmann: Bevölkerungsprojektionen für das wiedervereinigte Deutschland bis zum Jahr 2100. Institut für Bevölkerungsforschung und Sozialpolitik der Universität Bielefled, Bielefeld 1993

Bucher, Hansjörg; Kocks, Martina; Siedhoff, Mathias: Wanderungen von Ausländern in der Bundesrepublik Deutschland der 80er Jahre. In: Informationen zur Raumentwicklung, Heft 7/8, 1992, S. 501-511

Fleischer, Henning: Eheschließungen, Ehescheidungen, Geburten und Sterbefälle von Ausländern 1981. Wirtschaft und Statistik, 2/1983

Heilig, Gerhard; Büttner, Thomas; Lutz, Wolfgang: Germany's Population: Turbulent Past, Uncertain Future. in: Population Bulletin, Vol. 45, No. 4, December 1990, Washington

Herrmann, Helga: Ausländer: Vom Gastarbeiter zum Wirtschaftsfaktor. Beiträge zur Gesellschafts- und Bildungspolitik, 173, Institut der deutschen Wirtschaft, 2/1992

Meyer, Kurt; Paul, Christine: Allgemeine Sterbetafel 1986/88. Wirtschaft und Statistik 6/1991, S. 371ff

Proebsting, Helmut: Eheschließungen, Ehescheidungen, Geburten und Sterbefälle von Ausländern 1986. Wirtschaft und Statistik 2/1988

Schulz, Erika: Bevölkerungsentwicklung in Deutschland bis zum Jahr 2010 mit Ausblick auf 2040. Deutsches Institut für Wirtschaftsforschung - Wochenbericht; 29/93

Schulz, Erika: Szenarien der Bevölkerungsentwicklung in der Bundesrepublik Deutschland. Deutsches Institut für Wirtschaftsforschung - Wochenbericht; 8/90, 93-102

Schulz, Erika: Veränderte Rahmenbedingungen für die Vorausrechnung der Bevölkerungsentwicklung in der Bundesrepublik Deutschland. DIW Vierteljahres-berichte; 2/3, 1990, 169- 183

Schulz, Erika: Die Wanderungen ins Bundesgebiet seit 1984. DIW Diskussionspapiere Nr. 28. Deutsches Institut für Wirtschaftsforschung, Berlin 1991

Seifert, Wolfgang: Ausländer in der Bundesrepublik - Soziale und ökonomische Mobilität. AG Sozialberichterstattung, Wissenschaftszentrum Berlin für Sozialforschung, Berlin, Dezember 1991

Sommer, Bettina: Entwicklung der Bevölkerung bis 2030 - Ergebnis der siebten koordinierten Bevölkerungsvorausberechnung. <u>Wirtschaft und Statistik</u>, Heft 4, 1992, S. 217-222

Thränhardt, D. (ed.): <u>Europe - A new immigration continent</u>. Münster, Hamburg 1992

The Effects of Immigrants on the Income of Natives

Gunter Steinmann
Department of Economics
Martin-Luther University Halle-Wittenberg
Große Steinstr. 73
06108 Halle, Germany

1 Introduction

This paper studies the economic effects of immigration on the income of natives. We assume a world with flexible prices. The price reactions guarantee the full employment of all inputs at any time. Our model is a one sector growth model with two homogeneous inputs, capital K and labor L. The technology is described by the CES-production function:

(1) $\quad Y_t = A \cdot \left[\alpha K_t^{-\mu} + (1-\alpha) L_t^{-\mu} \right]^{-\frac{1}{\mu}}$

with $A > 0$ and $0 < \alpha < 1$.
The elasticity of substitution σ is determined by μ

$$\sigma = \frac{1}{1+\mu}$$

We consider the two cases $0 > \mu > -1$ $(\sigma > 1)$ and $\mu > 0$ $(\sigma < 1)$ and include the intermediate case $\mu = 0$ $(\sigma = 1)$ in our analysis. The intermediate case $\mu = 0$ leads to the Cobb-Douglas production function

(1a) $\quad Y_t = A \cdot K_t^{\alpha} L_t^{1-\alpha}$

We do not distinguish between labor and population and assume that natives and immigrants have identical labor qualities (homogeneous labor). Immigration does not begin before period $t = T$ and remains positive for all subsequent periods. Therefore, the population consists of natives Li in periods $t < T$ and of natives and non-natives La in later periods $t \geq T$. For simplicity, we assume that the ratio of non-natives to population is constant q.

(2)
$$La_t = qL_t$$
$$Li_t = (1-q)L_t$$
with $q = 0$ for $t > T$
$q > 0$ for $t \geq T$

The constant ratio of non-natives to population implies that total population and the number of natives and non-natives grow at the same rate n.

(3)
$$L_t = L_T(1+n)^{t-T}$$
$$Li_t = Li_T(1+n)^{t-T} \qquad t \geq T$$
$$La_t = La_T(1+n)^{t-T}$$

Aggregate income Y is the sum of the income of natives Yi and the income of non-natives Ya.

(4) $\quad Y_t = Yi_t + Ya_t$

The savings behaviour is described by

(5a) $\quad Si_t = si \cdot Yi_t \quad$ with $\quad 0 \leq si \leq 1$
(5b) $\quad Sa_t = sa \cdot Ya_t \qquad\qquad 0 \leq sa \leq 1$

The aggregate savings rate s is:

(5c)
$$s = \frac{S_t}{Y_t} = si \cdot \left(\frac{Yi_t}{Y_t}\right) + sa \cdot \left(\frac{Ya_t}{Y_t}\right)$$
$$= si \cdot \left(\frac{yi_t}{y_t}\right) \left(\frac{Li_t}{L_t}\right) + sa \cdot \left(\frac{ya_t}{y_t}\right) \left(\frac{La_t}{L_t}\right)$$

with $\quad yi_t = Yi_t/Li_t$, $\quad y_t = Y_t/L_t \quad$ and $\quad ya_t = Ya_t/La_t$.

The capital is owned partly by natives Ki and partly by non-natives Ka.

(6) $\quad K_t = Ki_t + Ka_t$

The amount of property the natives hold in the present time period depends upon the amount of property held and their savings behaviour in the previous period, as well as on the depreciation rate.

(7a) $\quad Ki_t = (1-d) \cdot Ki_{t-1} + si \cdot Yi_{t-1}$

The property of non-natives is additionally influenced by the amount of capital that the new immigrants brought into country from their home countries Ka_{t-1}^{im}.[1]

(7b) $\quad Ka_t = (1-d) \cdot Ka_{t-1} + sa \cdot Ya_{t-1} + Ka_{t-1}^{im}$

2 Short-run Effects of Immigrants on the Incomes of Natives

We restrict our analysis in this section to period T, the period immediately after the arrival of the immigrants (short-run effects). This period is short enough to assume that capital and technology are still unchanged by immigration. We also neglect the possibility that immigrants import capital $Ka_t^{im} = 0$. Consequently, immigrants neither own any capital in period T nor receive any profit or interest income. Profits and interest are completely earned by natives. Immigrants only receive wage income.

The assumption of flexible prices guarantees that immigration does not lead to unemployment but instead solely to lower wages and higher interest. Price changes have two opposite effects on the income of natives: they decrease wage income but increase interest income. Which effect is stronger? This question can be answered by the Cobb-Douglas-function.

The income of the natives YC_T is, in the absence of immigration, equal to the aggregate income Y_T.

(8a) $\quad YC_T = Y_T = A \cdot \left(\dfrac{K_T}{Li_T}\right)^\alpha \cdot Li_T$

An increase of the population (labor) by La_T immigrants leads to higher aggregate income (capital remaining unchanged). The income that is left over once the wage income of the immigrants has been substracted from aggregate income represents the new income of the natives Yi.

(8b) $\quad Yi_T = Y_T - w_T \cdot La_T = A \cdot \left(\dfrac{K_T}{L_T}\right)^\alpha L_T - A \cdot (1-\alpha) \cdot \left(\dfrac{K_T}{L_T}\right)^\alpha La_T$

with $L_T = Li_T + La_T$.

---

[1] We neglect all capital export and capital import other than Ka_{t-1}^{im} and assume that native-born testators leave their property to native-borns and foreign-born testators to foreign-borns.

From equations (8a) and (8b):

$$(9) \quad Yi_T > YC_T \quad \text{if} \quad \alpha \cdot \left(1 + \frac{La_T}{Li_T}\right) + (1-\alpha) \; > \; \left(1 + \frac{La_T}{Li_T}\right)^\alpha$$

Condition (9) holds whenever the number of immigrants is positive $La_T > 0$. The natives gain more from the higher interest income than they loose from the lower wage income. Furthermore, their short-run income gains increase as the number of immigrants increases.

It is often argued that immigrants impose costs on natives, such as the burden for supplying shelter to the new immigrants, the burdon of improving their education, etc. We can easily include these costs in our model. We may for, instance assume that the integration costs CI_T are positively related to the number of immigrants:

$$CI_T = a \cdot La_T^\Theta, \quad \text{with} \quad a > 0 \quad \text{and} \quad \Theta \geq 1$$

We calculate natives' income here by subtracting the immigrants' wage income and the integration costs from the aggregate income.

$$(8c) \quad Yi_T = Y_T - w_T \cdot La_T - CI_T = A \cdot \left(\frac{K_T}{L_T}\right)^\alpha \cdot L_T - (1-\alpha) \cdot \left(\frac{K_T}{L_T}\right)^\alpha La_T - a \cdot La_T^\Theta$$

From equations (8a) and (8c) we derive:

$$(9a) \quad Yi_T > YC_T \quad \text{if} \quad \alpha \cdot \left(1 + \frac{La_T}{Li_T}\right) + (1-\alpha) \; > \; \left(1 + \frac{La_T}{Li_T}\right)^\alpha + a \cdot \left[\frac{\left(\frac{La_T}{Li_T}\right)^\Theta}{\frac{Li_T^{1-\Theta} \cdot Y_T^\alpha}{L_T^\alpha}}\right]$$

Condition (9a) is fulfilled only by low values of a, Θ and La_T and high per capita income in the receiving country, i.e., if the integration costs are relatively low. Any integration costs for immigrants reduce their positive effects on the income of natives. Various simulations using other parameter values show that the introduction of integration costs makes immigration unprofitable to natives in nearly all cases, if only the short-run effects are used to determine our assessment while the long-run effects are neglected.

3 Long-run Effects of Immigrants on the Incomes of Natives

In section 2 we assumed that non-natives do not own capital and that natives, therefore, earn all profits and interest. This assumption is appropriate in the short-run during which immigrants have not yet been able to acquire any property, but it must be revised in the long-run, during which immigrants have saved part of their income and have become proprietors of domestic capital[2]. The immigrants then earn interest on their property and benefit from higher interest just as natives would. This effect is especially important when immigrants have spent a long period of time in their new country and have had a high savings ratio.

This section deals with the steady state equilibrium (long-run analysis). We alternatively assume the CES function with $\sigma = 1$ (Cobb-Douglas function) and the CES functions $\sigma > 1$ and $\sigma < 1$. We still ignore technical progress. The steady state growth rate is, therefore, equal to the long-run population growth rate n, which is assumed to be constant and unaffected by immigration (eq.2). The equilibrium capital-output ratio is determined by the savings rate and the rate of population growth

(10a) $\quad v = \dfrac{K}{Y} = \dfrac{s}{n}$

3.1 Cobb-Douglas-Production Function

Substituting the capital to labor ratio in eq.(1a) with eq.(10a) we arrive at the steady state solutions:

(10b) $\quad k = \dfrac{K}{L} = \left[A \cdot \dfrac{s}{n} \right]^{\frac{1}{1-\alpha}}$

(10c) $\quad y = \dfrac{Y}{L} = A \cdot \left[A \cdot \dfrac{s}{n} \right]^{\frac{\alpha}{1-\alpha}}$

The steady state income of the natives is determined assuming an absence of immigrants:

---

[2] The assumption only holds in the long-run in the unrealistic case where immigrants do not save but rather consume their full income.

(11a) $$YC = A \cdot \left[A \cdot \frac{si}{n} \right]^{\frac{\alpha}{1-\alpha}} \cdot Li$$

Immigration affects both the aggregate savings rate and the population size. Aggregate income with positive immigration is represented by the equation:

$$Y = A \cdot \left[A \cdot \frac{s}{n} \right]^{\frac{\alpha}{1-\alpha}} \cdot L$$

From this equation we can derive the income of natives Yi in an open economy:

(11b) $$Yi = \left(\frac{Yi}{Y} \right) \cdot A \cdot \left[A \cdot \frac{s}{n} \right]^{\frac{\alpha}{1-\alpha}} \cdot \left(\frac{L}{Li} \right) \cdot Li$$

and compare this income with the income of natives in the closed economy YC

(12) $$\frac{Yi}{YC} = \left(\frac{L}{Li} \right) \cdot \left(\frac{Yi}{Y} \right) \cdot \left[\frac{s}{si} \right]^{\frac{\alpha}{(1-\alpha)}}$$

The effects of immigration on the income of natives depends upon the amount of immigration (L/Li), the proportion of the natives' income to aggregate income (Yi/Y), the savings behaviour of natives and immigrants (s/si) and the production elasticities of capital and labor.

The steady state proportion of natives' income to aggregate income is[3]:

---

[3] The income of natives is defined as:
(i) $\quad Yi = w \cdot Li + r \cdot Ki$, with w: wage and r: interest rate.
If the factor prices of capital and labour are equal to their marginal products we get
(ii) $\quad Yi = (1-\alpha) \cdot (Y/L) \cdot Li + \alpha \cdot (Y/K) \cdot Ki$
where aggregate capital is the sum of the accumulated savings of the past (we disregard depreciation). In the same way we determine the stock of natives' capital by their accumulated savings:
(iii) $\quad K = \Sigma(s \cdot Y_t) \quad$ and $\quad Ki = \Sigma(si \cdot Yi_t)$
In a steady state Y and Yi grow by the same rate n. Consequently, the ratio of accumulated aggregate income and accumulated natives' income asymptotically approaches the ratio of period aggregate income to period income of natives:
(iv) $\quad \left[\Sigma Y_t / \Sigma Yi_t \right] \approx Y_t / \Sigma Yi_t$
(iii) and (iv) in (ii) yield:
(13) $\quad Yi/Y = \left[(1-\alpha)/(1 - \alpha \cdot si/s) \right] \cdot (Li/L)$

(13) $\quad \dfrac{Yi}{Y} = \dfrac{(1-\alpha)}{\left(1 - \dfrac{\alpha \cdot si}{s}\right)} \cdot \left(\dfrac{Li}{L}\right)$

In order for natives' income to be positive, it is required that:

(13a) $\quad \alpha < \dfrac{s}{si}$

We assume that this condition is satisfied.
(13) in (12) yields:

(14) $\quad \dfrac{Yi}{YC} = \dfrac{(1-\alpha)}{\left(1 - \alpha \cdot \dfrac{si}{s}\right)} \cdot \left[\dfrac{s}{si}\right]^{\frac{\alpha}{(1-\alpha)}}$

The steady state ratio of Yi to YC is directly determined by the production elasticities α, the savings rate of natives si and the aggregate savings rate s. The amount if immigration and the savings rate of non-natives indirectly influence the steady state ratio through their impact on the aggregate savings rate.

If non-natives and natives have identical savings rates $(si = sa)$, then natives neither benefit nor lose from immigration in the long-run:

(14a) $\quad Yi = YC$ if $s = si$, that is if $sa = si$ [eq.(5a)]

It is easy to interpret this result. In equilibrium, due to the given rate of population growth, the growth rate of aggregate income is unaffected by immigration. Therefore, the income of natives is only influenced by immigration if there are (1) changes in the functional income distribution, (2) wage differences between immigrants and natives or (3) changes in the aggregate savings rate and in the aggregate per capita income. The first possibility can be overlooked here, because the Cobb-Douglas production function does not allow changes in profit and wage shares. The second possibility is also excluded in our model, because the assumption of homogeneous labor implies identical wages for immigrants and natives. In this model, the only way in which immigrants can influence the income of natives is by the third possibility. When identical savings rates exist, the aggregate savings rate and the steady state aggregate per capita income are unaffected by immigration. Furthermore, discrepancies in immigrants' and natives' wealth disappear in the long-run if both groups have identical savings rates. This implies that, in the long-run immigrants and natives also receive the same amount of profits and, thus, cease to be economically distinct.

In the two other cases $(si < sa ; si > sa)$ the long-run income of natives is positively affected by immigration $(Yi > YC)$. This can be shown if we differentiate eq.(14):

$$\frac{\partial\left(\frac{Yi}{YC}\right)}{\partial\left(\frac{s}{si}\right)} = \left[\frac{(1-\alpha)}{\left(\frac{s}{si}\right)-\alpha}\right] \cdot \left[\frac{s}{si}\right]^{\frac{\alpha}{(1-\alpha)}} \cdot \left[1 - \frac{\left(\frac{s}{si}\right)}{\left(\frac{s}{si}\right)-\alpha} + \frac{\alpha}{1-\alpha}\right]$$

with $\partial(Yi/YC)/\partial(s/si) > 0$ if $sa > s > si$ and $\partial(Yi/YC)/\partial(s/si) < 0$ if $sa < s < si$ [notice that $\alpha < (s/si)$].

The ratio of Yi to YC is at its minimum $(Yi/YC = 1)$ if $sa = s = si$. In both other cases $(sa > si$ or $sa < si)$ Yi exceeds YC (see figure 1).

Therefore, positive immigration improves natives' long-run income, unless immigrants exhibit the same savings behaviour as natives. If non-natives save more than natives $(sa > si)$, aggregate per capita income, the aggregate savings rate, the capital-output ratio and the wage rate rise, while the interest rate falls. The relatively high savings rate of non-natives compared to the savings rate of natives supplies immigrants with more capital per person in the long-run than the natives have. Consequently, natives are harmed less by the decrease in interest rates than non-natives are, but natives are fully affected by the income and wage increases which result from increased savings. In this case, the natives benefit from immigration.

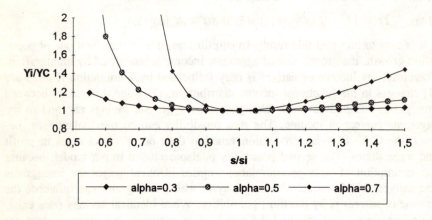

Figure 1: The long run effects of immigration on natives' incomes (Cobb-Douglas-Function)

On the other hand, if non-natives save less than natives $(sa < si)$, aggregate per capita income, the aggregate savings rate, the capital-output ratio and the wage rate fall, while the interest rate rises. The relatively low savings rate of non-natives in comparison to the savings rate of natives leads to results similar to those experienced in the short-run (immediately after the arrival of immigrants). Immigrants own less capital per person than the natives do, therefore, the natives gain more from the higher interest rate. The positive effect of higher interest on their income outweighs the negative income effects which result from lower wages and lower aggregate income.

3.2 CES-Production Function

The new steady state solution is [eq.(10a) in eq.(1)]:

$$(15) \quad \left(\frac{Y}{L}\right)^{\mu} = \frac{A^{\mu}}{(1-\alpha)} - \left(\frac{\alpha}{1-\alpha}\right) \cdot \left(\frac{n}{s}\right)^{\mu}$$

By comparing the steady state income of the closed economy (population Li, savings rate si) with the steady state income of the open economy (population $L = Li + La$, savings rate s is equal to the weighted average of si and sa), we get

$$(16a) \quad \frac{Y}{YC} = \left[\frac{(1-b)}{(1-bi)}\right]^{\frac{1}{\mu}} \quad \text{with}$$

$$(16b) \quad b = \left(\frac{\alpha}{A^{\mu}}\right) \cdot \left(\frac{n}{s}\right)^{\mu} \quad \text{and}$$

$$(16c) \quad bi = \left(\frac{\alpha}{A^{\mu}}\right) \cdot \left(\frac{n}{si}\right)^{\mu} = b \cdot \left(\frac{s}{si}\right)^{\mu} \quad bi = \left(\frac{\alpha}{A^{\mu}}\right) \cdot \left(\frac{n}{si}\right)^{\mu} = b \cdot \left(\frac{s}{si}\right)^{\mu}$$

A positive steady state income requires that $b, bi < 1$. We can transform eq.(16a) in:

$$(17) \quad \frac{Yi}{YC} = \frac{Yi \cdot L}{Y \cdot Li} \cdot \left[\frac{1-b}{1-b \cdot \left(\frac{s}{si}\right)^{\mu}}\right]^{\frac{1}{\mu}}$$

The steady state proportion of natives' income to aggregate income is shown by:[4]

---

[4] The income of natives is defined as:
(i) $Yi = w \cdot Li + r \cdot Ki$

(18) $$\frac{Yi}{Y} = \left(\frac{Li}{L}\right) \cdot \frac{(1-b)}{\left(1-b \cdot \frac{si}{s}\right)}$$

(18) in (17) yields:

(19) $$\frac{Yi}{YC} = F \cdot G$$

with $F = \left[\dfrac{1-b}{1-b \cdot \left(\dfrac{si}{s}\right)}\right]$ and $G = \left[\dfrac{1-b}{1-b \cdot \left(\dfrac{s}{si}\right)^{\mu}}\right]^{\frac{1}{\mu}}$

and the conditions for the existence of a positive steady state solution are:

(20) $$b < 1, \quad b \cdot \left(\frac{s}{si}\right)^{\mu} < 1, \quad b \cdot \left(\frac{si}{s}\right) < 1$$

The steady state ratio of Yi and YC is determined by the parameters of the production function (A, α, μ), the rate of population growth n, the savings rate of natives si and the aggregate savings rate S. The aggregate savings rate is, in turn, influenced by the proportion of non-natives to total population and their savings rate sa.

We again reach the conclusion that the natives neither benefit nor lose from immigration in the long-run if the non-natives exhibit the same savings behaviour as the natives. In the other two cases $(si > s > sa;\ si < s < sa)$ the consequences are less obvious at first sight, because $F < 1$ if $G > 1$ and $F > 1$ if $G > 1$.

(ii) $\quad w = \left[(1-\alpha)/A^{\mu}\right] \cdot (Y/L)^{\mu+1}$

(iii) $\quad r = \left[\alpha/A^{\mu}\right] \cdot (Y/K)^{\mu+1}$

(iii) in (ii) yields:

$Yi/Y = \left[(1-\alpha)/A^{\mu}\right] \cdot (Y/L)^{\mu} \cdot (Li/L) + \left[\alpha/A^{\mu}\right] \cdot (Y/K)^{\mu} \cdot (Ki/K)$

or in equilibrium:

(iv) $\quad Yi/Y = (1-b) \cdot (Li/L) + b \cdot (Ki/K)$ and

(v) $\quad Ki/K = (si/s) \cdot (Yi/Y)$

(iv) in (v) leads to eq.(18).

Table 1:

	$\mu > 0$	$\mu < 0$
$si > s$	$F > 1, \ G < 1$	$F > 1, \ G < 1$
$si = s$	$F = 1, \ G = 1$	$F = 1, \ G = 1$
$si < s$	$F < 1, \ G > 1$	$F < 1, \ G > 1$

(19a) $\quad Yi = YC \quad$ if $\quad si = s = sa$

What result do we get in the other two cases? We arrive at the answer by differentiating eq.(19) with respect to (s/si):

$$\frac{\partial\left(\frac{Yi}{YC}\right)}{\partial\left(\frac{s}{si}\right)} \begin{matrix}>\\=0\\<\end{matrix} \text{ if } \frac{b\cdot\left[\left(\frac{s}{si}\right)^{\mu+1}-1\right]}{\left[1-b\cdot\left(\frac{s}{si}\right)^{\mu}\right]\cdot\left[\left(\frac{s}{si}\right)-b\right]} \begin{matrix}>\\=0\\<\end{matrix}$$

We know from condition (20) that the denominator of the fraction in the bracket is positive. The numerator is negative if $sa < s < si$ and is positive if $sa > s > si$. Therefore

(19b) $\quad \dfrac{\partial\left(\dfrac{Yi}{YC}\right)}{\partial\left(\dfrac{s}{si}\right)} < 0 \text{ if } sa < s < si$

and

(19c) $\quad \dfrac{\partial\left(\dfrac{Yi}{YC}\right)}{\partial\left(\dfrac{s}{si}\right)} > 0 \text{ if } sa > s > si$

The results we obtain are identical to the results found using the Cobb-Douglas production function. The natives neither benefit nor lose from immigration $Yi/YC = $ if natives and non-natives have the same savings rate. In all other cases, the natives experience net gains due to immigration $Yi/YC > 1$. The extent of the benefits depends upon the elasticity of substitution and the savings rates of natives and non-nativs; they increase as the difference between s and si increases, i.e., they are positively related to the amount of immigration and to the discrepancy in the savings patterns of natives and non-natives.

The elasticity of substitution strongly affects the income gains of the natives. The higher the elasticity, the more favourable immigration is for the natives. It is not difficult to support this claim. If the savings rate of immigrants differs from the savings rate of natives, then immigration leads to a higher or lower steady state ratio between capital and labor, and will necessarily alter the functional income distribution, unless the elasticity of substitution is equal to 1 (Cobb-Douglas function).

Consider first the case of a relatively high elasticity of substitution $(\sigma > 1)$. In this case, the profit share on output is inversely related to the savings rate, i.e., the profit share increases if $sa < s < si$ and decreases if $sa > s > si$. The natives have, on the average, more (less) property than non-natives if $sa < s < si$ ($sa > s > si$). Consequently, natives gain from the redistribution of the functional incomes both for $sa < s < si$ and for $sa > s > si$. They benefit if immigration leads to capital scarcity [$sa < s < si$] and rising profit shares, because they own more capital than immigrants do. Natives also gain if immigration leads to capital affluence [$sa > s > si$] with falling profit shares, because in this case immigrants own more capital than the natives do. This process reinforces the redistribution process described in the last section which acts in favour of the natives with respect to the new aggregate savings rate and its effect on the wage rate and interest rate tendencies (see figure 2a).

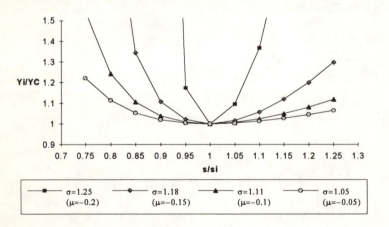

Figure 2a: The long-run effects of immigrants on natives' incomes for high elasticities of substitution $(\sigma > 1)$

The situation differs if the elasticity of substitution is relatively low $(\sigma < 1)$. In this case, the immigrants benefit from changes in the functional income, whereas the natives lose.

However, it is still true that changes in the wage rate and the interest rate positively affect the income of natives. Does a positive or negative income effect prevail? Our analysis shows that the natives are still better off with immigration, due to changes in factor prices. The natives' profits are, however, small and insignificant (see figure 2b). Only if the elasticity of substitution is relatively close to 1 and if immigrants strongly affect the aggregate savings rate, i.e. if we observe large scale immigration with vast differences in the savings rates of natives and immigrants, do the natives increase their steady state income by five percent or more (see figure 2c, notice the differences in the scales of the X-axis and the Y-axis compared to figures 2a and 2b!).

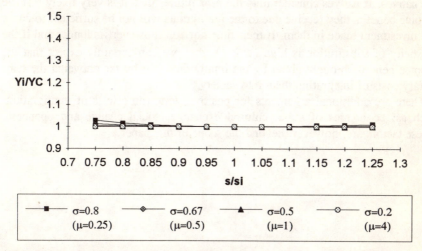

Figure 2b: The long-run effects of immigrants on natives´ incomes for low elasticities of substitution ($\sigma < 1$)

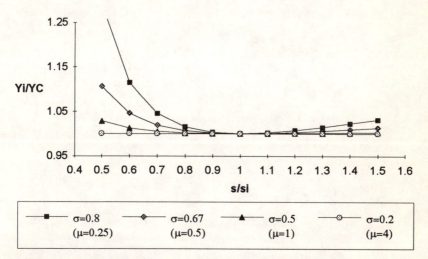

Figure 2c: The long-run effects of immigrants on natives´ incomes for high elasticities of substitution ($\sigma < 1$)

4 Conclusions

Our analysis shows that natives will benefit from immigration in the long-run in nearly all cases, but that, in the short-run, they will most likely be harmed by immigration. This is due to the "investment costs" (costs of integration) that natives are usually required to pay for some period of time to new immigrants. The assessment of immigrants' value, therefore, depends upon the time horizon of the natives. If natives consider only the near future, then it is very likely that the income benefits they receive due to the immigrants will not be sufficient to cover the investment made in them. If their time horizon, however, is longer and if the elasticity of substitution is high ($\sigma \geq 1$), then we can certainly expect that the income benefits brought about by the immigrants will by far outweigh the temporary costs of integrating them into society.

There are additional arguments for positive, long-run effects of immigration, such as: economics of scale, cultural exchange, social change and openness. These factors are, however, beyond the scope of this paper.

References

Berry, R.A.; R. Soligo: Some Welfare Aspects of International Migration, <u>Journal of Political Economy</u>, vol. 77, 1969, pp. 778-794.

Meier, V. and A. Wenig: <u>Welfare Implications of International Labor Migration</u>, Working Paper, University of Bielefeld, 1992

Simon, Julian L.: <u>The economic consequences of immigration</u>, Oxford and Cambridge, Mass., Blackwell in association with the Cato Institute, 1989, pp. xxxii, 402, 1989

Usher, Dan: Public Property and the Effects of Migration upon Other Residents of the Migrations Countries of Origin and Destination, <u>Journal of Political Economy</u>; 85(5), 1977, pp. 1001-20

Foreigners and the Social Insurance System in Germany[1]

Ralf E. Ulrich
Faculty of Social Sciences
Humboldt University Berlin
Unter den Linden 6
10099 Berlin, Germany

1 Introduction

Most West European countries have experienced high immigration and growing ratios of foreign-born residents among their populations in the last decades. The social security system is highly developed in this region. It redistributes a large part of the gross domestic product. Immigrants are often entitled to social security benefits and they pay contributions if they are gainfully employed. Immigrants are not totally homogeneous to natives in their socio-economic and demographic structure. Although it is obvious that they influence the social security system the direction of this influence is a priori not clear.

In public perception a negative impact of immigration on the public coffer in general is assumed. In a representative inquiry in 1982 German citizens were asked about their perceptions of foreigners. When asked "Is it true that foreigners with many children often come to Germany only because of the high subsidies for children?" 76 percent answered with "Yes" (Wiegand, 1984, p.13). There are only few scientific inquiries trying to verify these perceptions.

This paper deals with the direct impact of immigration on the system of social security in Germany. In a first part previous approaches to the problem are examined. In a second section methodological aspects of this question are discussed. Thirdly, micro-data from the German Socio-Economic Panel (SOEP) are used to make an estimate for 1984 and to identify important determinants. It is shown how the demographic and economic characteristics of immigrants determine their effects on public finances. Immigrants' features are specific in different host countries and they may change over time. In a final section, the impact of foreigners on unemployment insurance, public health insurance and the public pension system in Germanys are analysed in a dynamic view, using available macro-data. The paper comes to the result that labor migrants have been and are

---

[1] This paper is based on research supported by the German Research Foundation (DFG).

still an asset for the system of social security in Germany. But since this is now mainly the result of their juvenile age structure it might change in the future.

2 Previous Studies of the Subject

Studies on the impact of immigrants on social security and public households have a tradition in the US. In a recent article Rothman and Espenshade review 17 articles on this subject (Rothman/Espenshade, 1992).

An influential contribution has been made by Julian Simon (1977). He used micro-data from the 1976 Survey of Income and Education (SIE) to estimate tax payments and the use of social services for natives and immigrants in the US. He looked at the household level, since some transfer payments are addressed to the household rather than the individual. Simon included all natives in one group. He divided the immigrants into several groups, according to the year of their arrival in the US. He excluded those families from the analysis who immigrated before 1950, because they "... must now be seen as part of an ongoing system" (Simon, 1984, p. 59). After all, these families made up about half of all immigrant families. If they entered the US before 1950, it is obvious that they represent mainly the older age groups among the immigrants. Simon hence compares one group of natives representing all age groups with several groups of immigrants together representing the younger half of the immigrants.

Data on important transfer payments was included in the SIE sample, as well as income data. Simon roughly estimated the tax payments of various groups by multiplying their income with a "mean" tax rate of 29 percent. The effects of progressive taxation are therefore excluded. According to the SIE data the income of immigrants grew with the length of their stay in the US. Immigrants who had been in the US longer than four years and less than 25 had a higher income than the average natives. The cohorts that Simon excluded from the analysis had an average income below the average of natives. This is not surprising, since a great part of native families were in the pension age. According to Simons results the use of transfer payments by immigrants grows with the length of their stay in the US. The highest transfer payments were received from families who came to the US. before 1950.

Julian Simon's analysis comes to the result that immigrants contribute more to public households than they take from them. However, this result is only valid for the younger half of the immigrants that came to the US after 1950. In some way this result was already determined by the question Simon asked. If he considered on the immigrant side only the younger half while including on the natives side also the older half (with lower tax payments and higher use of transfer payments) no calculations were necessary to predict the result. This could be avoided by controlling for age.

Francine Blau (1984) used the same data set as Simon to compare transfer payments of immigrants and natives in the US. Blau differentiates between welfare payments and social insurance payments. The first are financed by tax payments, the second by fees. These two categories are also different in terms of eligibility requirements. Blau calculates the average use of transfer payments for all immigrants. Then the average transfers received by immigrant households are higher than those received by native households. Immigrant households with a male head received 50 percent more transfer payments than native households with a male head. In case of households headed by females the difference is not that large, but comparable.

Blau indicates that these differences were mainly determined by differences in the age structure of immigrants and natives. Within the same age groups immigrants received less transfer payments than natives. Blau explains the high share of older immigrants with the restrictive immigration policy of the United States during the 1920's.

The analysis by Ather Akbari (1989) for Canada is in line with Simon's method. Akbari uses data from the 1981 census. He shows that the income and the corresponding tax payments of immigrants grow with the duration of their stay in Canada. The average tax payments of all immigrants are higher than those of natives. On the other hand, on average, immigrants use more transfer payments than natives. The net balance of both factors - tax and transfer payments - is slightly positive. That means immigrants in Canada pay more in taxes than they receive in transfer payments.

Although Germany has a substantial foreign population of about six million, there are only few studies of their impact on public households available. Miegel (1984) and Wehrmann (1989) analysed this subject by use of macro-data and indirect estimates. They came to the result that today foreigners take more from the public treasury than they give. But in some areas their conclusions are to short-cut. They used the difference in unemployment rates between natives and foreigners to conclude directly to the use of unemployment benefits. A later section of this paper will show that this is not justified.

Gieseck/Heilemann/von Loeffelholz (1993) are dealing with the subject in a broader study on economic consequences of immigration to Germany. They used macro-data to make some rough estimates of additional tax revenues and expenditures due to immigration. Their main result is a positive impact of foreigners on public households. In their calculations they implicitly assumed that foreigners are homogeneous to Germans with regard to their average incomes, their labor force participation and their unemployment rate. This is obviously not the case. The impact of immigrants due to their specific position in the German labor market is therefore excluded from the view of the authors.

Bernhard Felderer deals with the problem in the context of a comparison between a pay-as-you-go system and a fully funded system. In line with the work of Ahlburg and Vaupel (1992) for the US he shows that extremely large immigration would be necessary to compensate the future demographic pressure on the pay-as-you-go system of social security in Germany. This result is based mainly on demographic simulations. Felderer implicitly assumes that the per capita contribution of immigrants is equal to natives.

3 Method of Analysis

The discussion of previous studies is leading to the basic approach of this paper. Obviously the analysis of macro-data has to be supported by the use of micro-data. This will allow a deeper insight into the differences between natives and foreigners with regard to contributions to the social security system on one side and the use of benefits on the other side. Studies for the US and other countries have shown the advantages of this approach. It had been not applied to Germany so far. Ideally, we would like to have a set of micro-data available for a longer time period to see things in development. The German Socio-Economic Panel seems to be such a data set. As will be shown later this does not apply to a significant comparison over time for this specific question. Therefore the SOEP data are used for a detailed analysis for one year only. This analysis will identify major determinants. Once the impact of these factors has been shown with micro-data it is easier to make indirect estimates for a period of time based on macro-data.

Several problems in methodology and data availability have to be discussed in advance.

An important determinant for the impact of immigration are legal regulations on the immigrants' entitlement to welfare transfers, on their contributions to the social security system and on their tax payments. Concerning these regulations there are *three groups of immigrants* in Germany.

- A first group are foreigners in Germany are *refugees*. Most of them came in, search of political asylum. A legal decision on their application can take years. A foreign population of 1.5 million refugees in different legal categories is estimated to live in Germany in the end of 1992. In the past the access of asylum seekers to the German labor market has been delayed for several years. After July 1991 asylum seekers can enter the labor market without any delay. But actually their labor force participation rate is very low. They are entitled to certain social welfare benefits, which are the basic source of their subsistence. Applicants for political asylum are clearly a burden for the public household, since they generally do not pay taxes or fees.
- A second group of immigrants are *labor migrants*. They constitute a foreign population of about 5 million people currently. Foreign workers are generally entitled to most of the social services which are available for Germans. On the other hand they pay taxes and social security fees like German citizens. The impact of this large group on public finances can only be evaluated by empirical estimates. The following part of this paper mainly concentrates on this group.

- A third group of immigrants are ethnic Germans from Eastern Europe (*Aussiedler*). They are German citizens and have the same rights and obligations as German "natives" after their arrival. This group is supported in their economic integration by substantial transfers. Gieseck/Heilemann/von Loeffelholz estimate 6 billion DM only in 1992 for the Aussiedler who immigrated 1988 to 1992 (1993, p. 37). Aussiedler are statistically almost invisible a few months after their arrival. Today they are not covered as a "stock" by official statistics, only as a "flow" when they arrive. There are only very few micro-data sets available on *Aussiedler*. That is why the impact of this group of immigrants could not be included in this paper.

Direct and indirect effects have to be distinguished when evaluating the impact of immigrants on the social security system. There are many indirect effects resulting from the impact on overall economic growth, the dynamics of wages and profits in the given tax system, etc. Several ways may be identified, in which immigration indirectly influences the public households in general and the social security system in particular. But some of these indirect effects are very speculative and it is nearly impossible to figure out how far they reach. This paper concentrates on the direct impact of foreigners on the system of social security in Germany.

For many of the indirect effects the actual number of immigrants is relevant. For the direct effects it is more the quality of immigrants, their age structure, labor force participation, unemployment rate, income level, etc. If immigrants were totally like natives their direct impact on public expenditures and revenues would be minor.

The demographic and economic structure of immigrants is specific to each host country. It is influenced by push and pull factors determining the migration stream and by its temporary or permanent character. Migrants are not the "average" citizen of their countries of origin. The push and pull factors result in a selection and self-selection of migrants. So we should not expect the same effects of immigration in all countries or at any time in history.

An important aspect is the *time scale* for an evaluation. Usually the balance is seen as the outcome of contributions and received transfers, i.e. in terms of current flows. This seems to be appropriate to unemployment insurance and public health insurance. It is obviously inappropriate for the pension insurance system. Here entitlements are accumulated during one period, while paying contributions. Services are received decades later, after entering the pension age. This has to be considered when comparing current contributions and payments. But changes in the age structure of immigrants are influencing also the health insurance. A long term view is needed here too. Demographic projections for the foreign population have been conducted to asses their future age structure and its impact.

4 An Estimate with SOEP Micro-Data

The Socio-Economic Panel is a longitudinal sample survey conducted annually in Germany. It contains representative micro-data on persons, families and households. The panel started in 1984, questioning about 6,000 households with more than 12,000 persons in Germany. Immigrants from the main "guest"-worker nationalities (Turkish, Greek, Italian, Yugoslavian and Spanish) were over-represented in the panel, with together 1,415 households in 1984. The intention was to allow conclusions not only for foreign workers as a group but also for the main nationalities themselves. Foreigners with other nationalities like American, Austrian or Polish were included in the "Germans" group. There are no representative data for these nationalities in the panel.

Ideally, we would like to compute results for all eight years covered by the SOEP so far. This would allow conclusions about some changes in this period. Most panels have the problem of panel mortality: during the years the number of continuing respondents is declining. There are some estimation techniques available to control for this problem. But the number of cases should be always large enough to get significant results. Unfortunately this is not given in our case.

Social security fees are paid only by a fraction of households, for example not by most students or pensioners. So, the number of valid cases is here much smaller than the total number of respondents. For some transfer payments (like unemployment benefits) the absolute number of cases is even much lower. For the first year a test of ONEWAY variance had shown that averages for the natives and foreigners subgroups were significantly different. Unfortunately this has been proved to be not given for the following years. The number of responding households in some categories became very small in the years after 1984. For the later years the average for some categories of transfer payments would have to be calculated on the base of only a few dozen households. ONEWAY calculations showed that the averages for natives and foreigners were not significantly different. The standard deviation within the subgroups was higher than within the entire dataset. Calculations for the later years of SOEP would not lead to serious results for the different types of transfers. Therefore this analysis had to be limited to the year 1984, with the maximum number of respondents. The results have been successfully tested for significance.

The questions of the panel cover a wide area: composition of households, labor force participation, occupational structure and mobility, income, education, health, use of disposable time, etc. Questions on different sources of income and different transfer payments received were included. There was a good coverage for some kinds of transfer payments, while for other types there was a rather high incidence of missings, or "Not available" answers. The explicit responses to questions on tax payments have been shown to be partly inconsistent. Many respondents could not recall properly their tax payments made one year ago. This was a reason to develop micro-simulation models to calculate consistent synthetic data.

A group of researchers at the Sonderforschungsbereich 3 at Frankfurt University constructed a micro-simulation model for the SOEP data (Berntsen, 1989). This model calculates social security fees for each respondent according to his income by applying the German regulations. Some of the data gaps on transfer payments are filled by the model, considering factors on the eligibility of respondents for certain payments. The synthetic data of the SOEP micro-simulation model for 1984 has been used in this analysis to estimate the contributions to the social security system and the transfer payments to Germans and foreigners.[2]

For a few households important information was not available. They had to be excluded to keep the sample consistent. The micro-data estimates for this analysis are calculated on a sample of 5,269 households with 10,310 adult persons. German and foreign households were grouped according to the head of the household.

Table 1 gives an overview of the main results of the micro-data calculations on household level.[3] The results of the calculations show that foreign households paid higher contributions to the social security insurance than Germans but received less of the observed transfers.

Table 1: Contributions to the social security insurance, tax payments and transfers, DM per average household, 1984

	Germans	Foreigners
Social security contributions	4,249	6,550
Unemployment insurance	560	874
Health insurance	1,435	2,159
Pension insurance	2,254	3,517
Selected transfers received:	6,380	1,505
Unemployment benefits	463	1,140
Pensions	5,917	365
memo:		
Tax payments:	8,050	7,129
Income tax	6,033	5,266
Value added tax	2,018	1,863

Calculations with SOEP data, except *) data from Statistisches Bundesamt; earlier published in Ulrich, 1992

---

[2] The author thanks Mr. Berntsen for his kind support.

[3] As already mentioned, the average figures given for foreigners and Germans have been tested to be significantly different (below the 0.001 level).

According to these data the German average household paid 4,249 DM in social security fees in 1984. The average foreign household paid 6,550 DM fees in the same year. The relation is different in case of tax payments. In this case foreigners reached only 89 percent of Germans' payments. The differences are greater for the progressive income tax than for the degressive value added tax.

The unemployment benefits received in average by foreign households are much higher than the average for Germans. Just the opposite is true in case of pensions. Summing up the average benefits from pension and unemployment insurance foreigners take far less in benefits than Germans. No data is available on the transfers received from the public health insurance system. Some indirect estimates on the position of Germans and foreigners are made in section 5.2.

From previous studies and common sense we know that differences in the age and employment structure and in the economic performance are responsible for the observed discrepancies. But how much do these factors contribute to the differences?

Chart 1 controls for the effect of age and employment status since it shows contributions to the social security system for five-year age groups of fully employed persons. It is obvious that the differences between Germans and foreigners are very small in this view. The differences in each age group are within the range of 8 percent.

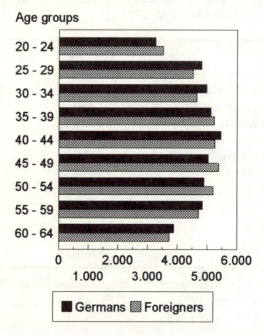

Calculations with SOEP data

Chart 1: Contributions to Social Security 1984, in DM, only fully employed persons

In order to estimate the isolated effect of the difference in age and employment structure another set of calculations have been done (Table 2). This time transfers were calculated on the personal level. By calculating average transfers for five-year age groups it was possible to standardise foreigners transfer payments to the age structure of Germans. The values in the third column of table 2 have to be read for the example of unemployment insurance fees as:

$$UBF_G = \frac{\sum_i UBF_i * PG_i}{PG_{total}}$$

where UBF_G is the average unemployment fee paid by foreigners if they would have the age structure of Germans, UBF_i is the unemployment contribution of foreigners in the five-year age group i, PG_i is the size of the age group i among Germans and PG_{total} is sum of population in all German age groups.

Table 2: Transfer Payments in DM per Person, 1984

	Germans	Foreigners unstandard.	standardised Age Structure	standardised Employment Structure
Contributions to the social security system				
Unemploym. Insurance	298	444	339	317
Health Insurance	765	1096	858	786
Pension Insurance	1,201	1,786	1,365	1,276
Received Transfer Payments				
Unemployment Benefits	248	584	456	445
Pensions	3,203	185	1181	271

Calculations with SOEP data

The same procedure has been applied to the employment status. Again the share of empoyment status groups among Germans was applied to the group specific averages of foreigners.

Average payments have been calculated for the following groups:
- fully employed
- part time employed
- unemployed
- not gainfully employed.

Table 2 shows main results. The contributions of foreigners to the social security system would have been substantially lower in 1984, if they had the age structure of Germans. This effect is even stronger if the employment structure of Germans would have been applied. As expected the average pensions received by foreigners would be much higher if they had the age structure of Germans.

These calculations confirm for Germany the important effect of age and employment structures of immigrants for the host country. Unfortunately the standardisation method can control only for each factor individually and not for both factors together. On the other hand age and employment structure are interrelated.

It is mainly their juvenile age structure and the higher labor force participation of foreigners what made them an asset for the social security system. These factors overcompensate the lower average income of foreigners up to now. Since it was not possible to include all kinds of transfers this picture is far from complete. But the transfers included in this analysis constitute a major part of all transfers.

5 Major Components and Determinants - A Dynamic Perspective

In the following section of this paper the three main parts of social security insurance are discussed on the base of macro-data. The main aim is to get an idea how important factors determining the impact of foreigners have changed in the past and how they might change in the future.

As already mentioned macro-data allow only indirect estimates. In the parts of the social security system the net balance for each subgroup (natives/immigrants) depends obviously on the following factors:

- the share of households paying fees or taxes or receiving benefits compared with all households in the subgroup. In other words: the average probability to pay fees or to receive benefits among Germans and foreigners.
- the average amount of fees or benefits per paying or receiving household.

The average risk to pay fees or to receive benefits is determined by different factors in the parts of the social security system respectively, as is the average amount of fees or payments.

5.1 Unemployment Insurance

Unemployment insurance payments are strictly proportional to the contributions paid by each individual. So, the average amount of payments per recipient and the average amount of contributions can cause no difference between natives and immigrants. If there are differences between Germans and foreigners they should result from the probability of receiving unemployment benefits.

Chart 2 shows the unemployment rate for all employees and for foreigners in Germany between 1960 and 1992. Until 1973 the unemployment rate of foreigners was always below the unemployment rate of Germans. Later on the unemployment rate was permanently higher among foreigners than among Germans. There are several reasons for this.

A first reason is the reaction of foreign labor to unemployment after the modification in the official German policy toward foreign workers in 1973. Before, foreign workers often went back to their home countries in the case of unemployment and returned when the situation on the labor market had improved. After the so-called recruitment stop this became risky for foreign workers from non-EEC countries. Once back in their country of origin, they could not be sure to have a chance to return to Germany, even if the labor market were to recover. Under these conditions the share of unemployed foreign workers who returned home remained much lower than before 1973. The share of unemployed foreign workers registered in Germany went up.

But the higher unemployment of foreigners in the last two decades has also more substantial reasons. Usually immigrants cannot fully transfer their human capital with migration. Beside the language barrier there are incompatibilities in professional profiles etc. The average level of general education and professional education of foreigners in Germany is below the native level. In the fifties and sixties there was a good matching between the educational and professional profiles of the "guest" workers and the need of the German labor market for unqualified labor. Foreign employees in Germany are traditionally concentrated in certain branches. But these branches have been most heavily affected by recession and structural change (Dietz 1987, Bach 1987). The secular change in the German economy favours branches in the tertiary sector requiring a higher educational level. In aggregate more jobs have been created in the tertiary sector than lost in primary and secondary sector. But this is not true for foreign workers. 519 thousand foreigners employed in manufacturing and another 137 thousand foreign workers employed in construction lost their job between 1974 and 1991. But in the tertiary sector only 124 thousand foreigners could find a new job. While the overall number of employees increased in this period by 2.2 million, the number of foreign employees decreased by 489 thousand. In other words: the increased unemployment of foreigners reflects their gradual displacement from the German labor market.

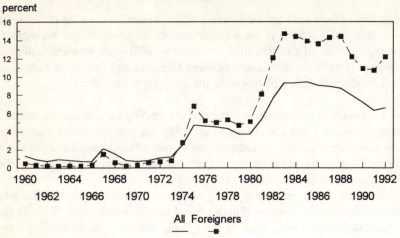

Chart 2

The boom induced by the German unification has only for a short moment modified the picture. Foreigners unemployment rate decreased from 12.2 percent in 1989 to 10.9 percent in 1990, but reached again 12.2 percent in 1992. The absolute number of registered unemployed foreigners climbed by 22.2 percent from 1991 to 1992.

The higher unemployment among foreigners after 1973 suggests that the share they receive from the unemployment insurance is larger than that of the Germans. This has been concluded by Miegl (1984) and Wehrmann (1989). But it is not necessarily true, since the risk to be unemployed is not identical with the probability to receive unemployment benefits. Employees are entitled to receive unemployment benefits only after a certain period of contribution payments before unemployment, usually one year. For Germans this is only relevant at the beginning of their professional career. Because of the high fluctuation of foreign workers, the proportion of people paying contributions but still being not entitled to receive benefits in the case of unemployment is large. Actually the share of unemployed who don't receive benefits is much higher among foreigners than among Germans. In 1984 it was 28 percent of unemployed among Germans, but 37 percent among foreigners (Bach, 1987, p. 171).

It is obvious that until 1973 foreign workers paid more contributions to the unemployment insurance than they took benefits from it - because their unemployment rate was lower than the Germans'. The SOEP micro-data showed for 1984 foreigners took more from the unemployment insurance than they paid in contribution. Evidence on the changed position of foreigners on German labor market and their high unemployment suggests that this relation is still remaining.

5.2 Public Health Insurance

Health insurance is different from unemployment insurance because it also covers people who do not pay contributions: members of the family of the contributor. The benefits in case of illness are independent from the amount of contributions paid in the past. In Germany this is called the "solidarity principle" of public health insurance. The potential factors that could determine a difference between Germans and foreigners are: the relation between the number of contributors and eligible persons, the average amount of contributions, the share of ill people and the average costs. For none of these factors direct macro data are available.

In the sixties many foreign workers came to Germany without their families. The foreign population had a specific age and sex structure, with a high share of single persons. So, we can assume that there were fewer family members entitled to health insurance benefits without paying contributions themselves. Chart 3 shows the share of foreigners in the population, among employees and among the contributors to the public health insurance. Even at the end of the sixties the share of foreigners among contributors was more than double of their share in the population, i.e. among potential receivers. During the seventies, when more and more foreign workers brought their families to Germany, these figures approached one another.

The second factor on the contributions side is the average amount of income, which determines the size of contributions. Data from SOEP and from several other sources (for example Rehfeld, 1991) show that the average income of foreigners in Germany is lower than that of Germans. Section 4 had estimated average contributions to the health insurance per household. This includes both effects: the number of contributors in the population and the average income. In 1984 German households paid 1626 DM, while foreign households paid 2337 DM. This difference is basically due to the higher share of older people among Germans, who do not pay health insurance contributions any more or much less.

If foreigners pay more contributions than Germans, what about their use of services ? Chart 4 shows the share of health insured employees who are unfit for work. Until the mid seventies this figure was lower among foreigners, later it became increasingly unfavourable for them. There is a controversy about the reasons for this development (Land, 1984). However, Wehrmann (1989) concluded from these figures that foreigners receive more services from the health insurance than Germans. But this depends not only on the share of ill people, but also on the cost of the respective medical treatments.

For Germany Camphausen (1983) has shown that the costs of a medical treatment are highly age-dependent. If older people get ill, their treatment is on average much more expensive than in the case of younger people. Since the foreign population in Germany is much younger than the German one, this should have an effect on the receipt of health services. Chart 5 shows age-specific shares of the overall costs in the health system and the share of the foreign population in the respective age groups. Foreigners are over-represented in younger groups which cause only a small share of the overall costs. Among those age-groups with the higher cost share foreigners are under-represented. If the costs in the health system were distributed only according to the age structure, the average foreigner would cause costs of 964 DM, an average German 1,470 DM in 1984.

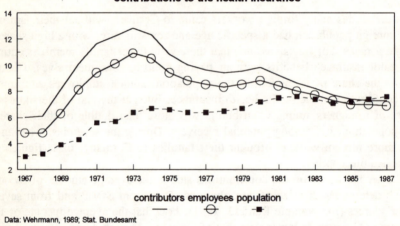

Share of foreigners of total population, of employees and of persons paying contributions to the health insurance

contributors   employees   population

Data: Wehrmann, 1989; Stat. Bundesamt

Chart 3

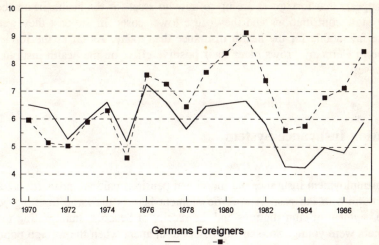

Chart 4

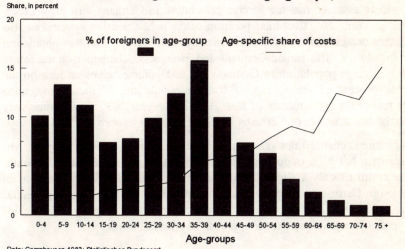

Chart 5

Although it is impossible to make a sound estimate that links all different aspects, it appears that foreigners are up to now an asset for the health insurance. They pay more contributions and they cause lower costs. In the past they were even more favourable for the health insurance than today. As far as the foreign population in Germany grows older their positive effect on the health insurance will decrease.

5.3 Pension Insurance System

Like in unemployment insurance the individual pensions paid are proportional to the contributions in the past. A specific moment here is the large time lag between the payment of contributions and the receipt of benefits. Immigrating foreign workers were young. So, starting from the moment when the foreign population in Germany began to grow, its impact was only on contributions. During this period and still recently they are obviously a positive factor. Decades later these people will cause costs for the pension insurance system.

Rehfeld (1991, p.491) has calculated contributions and pensions for Germans and foreigners for 1989. With 12.8 billion DM foreigners paid 7.8 percent of all contributions. They received 3.7 billion DM in pensions - 1.9 percent of all pensions paid. The surplus of 9.1 billion DM paid in contributions by foreigners could be used to finance pensions for Germans. That was about a fourth of the transfers from tax financed public households to the pension insurance system.

It is widely assumed that the foreign population in Germany will grow older. This will substantially affect their position in the public pension system but also in the other branches of the social security system. Official German population projections do not differentiate Germans and foreigners. The paper on the future growth of foreign population in Germany (in this volume) gives an idea on the inevitable process of the ageing of foreign population. If these projections become reality the age structure of foreigners in the year 2030 would come very close to the age structure of Germans in 1984. This can be seen in Chart 6.

This picture is changed not very much if the future immigration is higher. Another scenario has been calculated with 200 thousand net immigration annually with the result of only a slightly younger age structure. Inevitably the foreign population in Germany will grow older in the future - if there is no exponential increase in immigration. The very young age structure of foreigners in the sixties and seventies was a unique situation, a kind of windfall profit.

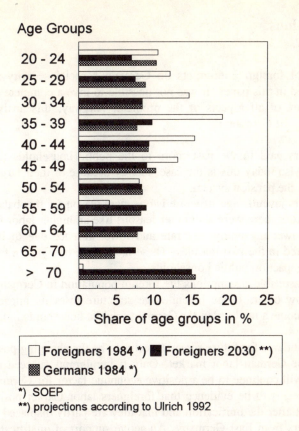

Chart 6: Age Structure: Germans and Foreigners

The growing share of foreigners among pensioners can already be seen today. At the beginning of 1991 the share of foreigners among all pensioners was 5.3 percent, while their share among new pensioners in 1990 was 9.4 percent (Rehfeld, 1991, p. 487).

The simulations show that the positive effect of foreigners on the pension insurance system is of a temporary nature. It will be gradually reduced in the next years. This would even be the case if there were a continued net immigration on the average level of the sixties, like assumed in one scenario. The surplus of foreigners' contributions in the past allowed to establish a level of pensions today that will be difficult to maintain in the future. So, for the pension insurance system the redistribution between generations seems to be more important in the long run than a potential redistribution between Germans and foreigners.

6 Conclusions

The effects of foreign immigrants on Germany's social security system have been discussed in this paper. It was not possible to give a complete and comprehensive picture of all aspects of the problem. Anyway, this analysis came to certain results for Germany:

- Foreigners paid in the past more to the public households than they received. Also today this is the case, mainly because of their large net contribution to the pension system.
- Foreigners juvenile age structure is one main reason for this balance.
- In the sixties there were also other reasons like an higher labor force participation, lower unemployment rate and lower absence due to illness. They disappeared in the past decades. These factors are now not in favour of foreigners impact on public households.
- Given reasonable assumptions the foreign population in Germany will inevitably grow older. If the juvenile age structure loses its impact foreigners might become a net burden for Germanys public households in the future.

An important area for future research seems to be the changing position of foreigners on the German labor market. Only if immigrants succeed on the labor market they will continue to be a positive economic factor for Germany as in the past. There seems to be evidence that foreigners labor market position became more difficult after the unification and that they are partly displaced by migrants and commuters from East Germany. An active support of qualification and language training for foreign workers - like it has been granted for immigrants of German ethnic (Aussiedler) - might prove to be a good investment.

References

Ahlburg, D.; J. W. Vaupel: Immigration and the dependency burden. Paper presented at the Internationl Conference on Mass Migration in Europe, Vienna 1992

Akbari, Ather H. : The Benefits of Immigrants to Canada: Evidence on Tax and Public Services.. Canadian Public Policy; 15(4), December 1989, pages 424-35., 1989

Bach, H.-U.: Entwicklung und Struktur der Ausländerarbeitslosigkeit in der Bundesrepublik Deutschland. In: Aspekte der Ausländerbeschäftigung in der Bundesrepublik Deutschland. Nürnberg 1987

Barth, Siegrun; Hain, Winfried: Demographie und Rentenversicherung - Langfristige Vorausrechnungen zu den Rentenfinanzierungen. Deutsche Rentenversicherung; 10-11, 1991, 724-739, 1991

Berntsen, Roland: Einkommensanalysen mit den Daten des Sozio-ökonomischen Panels unter Verwendung von generierten Einkommensdaten.. Sfb 3-Arbeitspapier Nr. 291. Frankfurt - Mannheim, 1989

Blau, Francine D.: The Use of Transfer Payments by Immigrants. Industrial and Labor Relations Review; 37(2), January 1984, pages 222-39., 1984

Camphausen, Bernd: Auswirkungen demographischer Prozesse auf die Berufe und die Kosten im Gesundheitswesen. Springer Verlag: Berlin, Heidelberg, New York, 1983

Deiniger, Dieter: Sozialhilfeempfänger 1988. Wirtschaft und Statistik; 6/1990, 1990

Dietz, F.: Entwicklung und Struktur der beschäftigten ausländischen Arbeitnehmer in der BRD. In: Aspekte der Ausländerbeschäftigung in der Bundesrepublik Deutschland. Nürnberg 1987

Felderer, Bernhard: Immigration and the social security system. mimeo 1992

Gieseck, Arne; U. Heilemann; H. D. von Loeffelholz: Wirtschafts- und sozialpolitische Aspekte der Zuwanderung in die Bundesrepublik. Aus Politik und Zeitgeschichte, B7 1993,

Greenwood, Michael J.; McDowell, John M.: The Factor Market Consequences of US. Immigration. Journal of Economic Literature; 24(4), December 1986, pages 1738-72., 1986

Kaiser, Helmut: Die Mehrwertsteuerbelastung privater Haushalte in der Bundesrepublik Deutschland. DIW-Vierteljahresberichte, Heft 1, 1989

Kassella, Thomas: Die Konstruktion eines synthetischen Mikrodatenfiles für steuerpolitische Simulationen. Sfb 3-Arbeitspapier Nr. 266. Frankfurt - Mannheim, 1988

Land, F.-J.: Zur Hypothese vom "Mißbrauch der Krankenversicherung" durch ausländische Arbeitnehmer. Soziale Sicherheit 4/1984

Miegel, Meinhard: Arbeitsmarktpolitik auf Irrwegen. Bonn 1994

Rehfeld, U.: Ausländische Arbeitnehmer und Rentner in der gesetzlichen Rentenversicherung. Deutsche Rentenversicherung 7/1991, S. 468-492, 1991

Rosenberg, P.: <u>Das soziale Netz vor der Zerreißprobe?</u> Frankfurt/M. 1990

Rothman, E.S.; Th. J. Espenshade: Fiscal impacts of immigration to the United States. <u>Population Index</u> 58(3), Fall 1992

Simon, Julian L. : <u>The economic consequences of immigration</u>. Oxford and Cambridge, Mass.: Blackwell in association with the Cato Institute, 1989., pages xxxii, 402., 1989

Simon, Julian L.: Immigrants, Taxes, and Welfare in the United States.. <u>Population and Development Review</u>; 10(1), March 1984, pages 55-69., 1984

Simon, Julian: <u>What immigrants take from, and give to the public coffers</u>. Illinois 1980, mimeo

Ulrich, Ralf: Der Einfluß der Zuwanderung auf die staatlichen Einnahmen und Ausgaben in Deutschland. <u>Acta Demographica</u>, 1992

Usher, Dan: Public Property and the Effects of Migration upon Other Residents of the Migrants' Countries of Origin and Destination. <u>Journal of Political Economy</u>; 85(5), October 1977, pages 1001-20., 1977

Wehrmann, Martin: <u>Auswirkungen der Ausländerbeschäftigung auf die Volkswirtschaft der Bundesrepublik Deutschland in Vergangenheit und Zukunft</u>. Baden-Baden 1989

Wiegand, Erich: Die <u>Inanspruchnahme ausgewählter Sozialleistungen durch Ausländer</u>. Ergebnisse der Ausländerumfrage 1982. Arbeitspapier Nr. 134. Sonderforschungsbereich 3. J. W. Goethe-Universität Frankfurt und Universität Mannheim, 1984

Wiegand, Erich: Zunahme der Ausländerfeindlichkeit ? Einstellung zu Fremden in Deutschland und Europa. <u>ZUMA-Nachrichten</u> 31, Jg. 16, November 1992

Blue Collar Labor Vulnerability: Wage Impacts of Migration

John P. De New
SELAPO, University of Munich
Ludwigstrasse 28 RG
80539 Munich, Germany

Klaus F. Zimmermann
SELAPO, University of Munich and CEPR, London
Ludwigstrasse 28 RG
80539 Munich, Germany

1 Introduction

There have always been concerns about the labor market consequences of immigration. In Germany, with the open borders of the European Community, this debate has gained the ever-increasing attention of politicians and employees alike. Are there costs and/or benefits to increased immigration for the host country? Are some job groups or industries affected more than others or are these effects shared equally across the economy? Most economists support the position, that for allocative reasons, free international movements of labor are beneficial for the economy as a whole, as is the free movement of capital and goods. This judgement is based on the standard competitive model of labor migration. However, native labor may be adversely affected and with increasing unemployment prevalent in the host country, increased immigrant labor may be politically and fiscally undesirable.

A key issue for the evaluation of the wage effects of immigrant labor is whether foreigners are subsitutes or complements to natives. A reasonable simplification is that high-qualified and low-qualified workers are complements, and immigrants tend to be substitutes to low-qualified natives and complements to high-qualified natives. Specifically, foreigners would be then substitutes for those Germans with a low level of education, as firms would be indifferent between these foreigners and their German counterparts. Conversely, those Germans with the necessary high level of training/skills/education would typically be in positions of middle and higher rank of some nature, requiring this higher level of skill. They could act as complements to the relatively under-educated foreigners. One would then expect, all things being equal, that the wages of the relatively scarce better qualified, would be positively affected by the inflow of underskilled foreigners. By the same line of reasoning, those Germans under-educated, and competing with foreigners for those jobs requiring little skill, would have their wage levels adversely affected by the same foreigners. This paper explores the issue of how wages of blue collar workers are affected using a vast micro panel data set for West Germany from 1984 to 1989.

Section 2 outlines the theoretical framework and provides a survey of the recent literature. Section 3 explains the data and summarizes the econometric approach. Section 4 presents the empirical results. Section 5 concludes.

2 Research Strategy and Review of Recent Findings

The issue of substitutability is often seen as central to the evaluation of the threat of immigration. This concept is based on the theory of production with multiple factor inputs which is well described in Hamermesh (1986). Within this approach, natives and foreigners can be seen as potentially different factors of production. Two factors are considered to be q-complements if an increase in the use of one factor affects the productivity of the other factor positively. Both factors are seen as q-substitutes if the productivity of one factor declines when the quantity of the other factor used in production is increased.

A simple extension in this framework is to consider quantity and quality of labor (hours worked and level of education) as factors of production. It is often then hypothesized that these factors are q-complements. Immigrants then provide quantity and quality of labor, and it depends on the composition of the inflow whether the impact is positive or negative for the natives. (For an elaboration of such a framework see Winkelmann and Zimmermann (1993).). Immigrants to West Germany in the last decades were primarily low educated. It is therefore an accurate framework to assume that there are basically two educational groups with low or high level of education. Immigrants then are subsitutes to low educated natives, and they can be (as the low educated natives) be complements to the better educated natives. It is then possible that immigration causes a threat to low income groups but increases the earnings of the higher income groups.

A simple labor market model demonstrates the discussed effect of incoming new workers. Figure 1 illustrates the different labor market equilibria for low and high skilled employees. While the demand for low-skilled workers is given by L^d_l, these workers supply L^s_l, resulting in the equilibrium l. Analogously, the equilibrium h for high-skilled workers is given by the intersection of demand L^d_h, and supply L^s_h. Migration by foreign workers, who are typically assumed to be low-skilled, add to the supply of low-skilled German workers, pushing the L^s_l curve to $L^{s'}_l$, thereby unambiguously decreasing the equilibrium low-skilled wage to l'. If the high-skilled employees are complements to the low-skilled, this influx of foreign low-skilled labor likely increases the demand for high-skilled labor, shifting the demand L^d_h to $L^{d'}_h$. The new equilibrium h' implies an increase in the wage for high-skilled labor.

There are basically two approaches to follow in empirical research. A production function can be estimated using quantity and quality variables of labor. After examining the quality content of the inflow of migrants, one can simulate the potential effects on native labor. In this simulation, one has to make difficult assumptions about the measurement of education and about the equivalence of foreigners in the production process. A different approach is to directly examine the effect of foreigners on the productivity of natives. This is the framework applied in this paper.

The effect of the share of foreigners in each of the major industries in West Germany is examined in the rest of the paper. The higher this share, the more positive the effect on the high-skilled wage is expected to be. Similarly, the consequences of an increasing share produce a downward pressure on the low-skilled wage. In the empirical analysis, we differentiate between labor market experience and job-status, and separating the sample into experienced and inexperienced laborers to allow for a more sophisticated pattern of labor relations.

Before we investigate the issue further, we provide a brief survey of related studies in the literature. The effects of foreign employment on both wages and unemployment are considered in the literature. As Greenwood and McDowell (1986) and Straubhaar and Zimmermann (1992) summarize, most of the effects are negative but surprisingly small. However, most of these studies are for the US. For instance, LaLonde and Topel (1991) do not find relevant effects on earnings and employment of natives. Altonji and Card (1991) received only a small competitiveness between low educated natives and immigrants. Winegarden and Khor (1991) find only negligable effects of illegal immigrants on natives. One explanation for these results can be seen in the low qualification of recent immigrant waves to the US.

More critical is a recent contribution of Borjas, Freeman and Katz (1991). They start from the stylized fact that wages and employment rates of less-skilled Americans fell relative to those of more-skilled workers in the 1980s. They argue that this development is related to an increase of the supply of less-skilled workers induced by trade and immigration. An effective supply of high-school dropouts of 28% for men and 31% for women was found to be caused by trade and immigration, which also affected adversely relative earnings of this group.

It is largely debated whether foreigners and natives are primarily substitutes or complements. Rivera-Batiz and Sechzer (1991) find that education, experience and quantity of labor are complements, but there are objections. (See Akbari and Devoretz (1992), for instance.) It is also questionable whether these results can be used to examine the relationships between foreigners and natives. Direct support for the hypothesis of complementarity can be found in Borjas (1983, 1986). Controversial and more critical findings are contained in Smith and Newman (1977), Defreitas and Marshall (1983), Matta and Popp (1985), Davila and Mattila (1985), Bean, Lowell and Taylor (1988) and Taylor, Bean, Rebitzer, Gonzalez-Baker and Lowell (1988).

For Germany, the empirical findings are still rather scarce. An early study by Spitznagel (1987) found no effects of the share of foreigners in the industries on wages. Wehrmann (1989) found negative employment effects of foreigners. Barabas, Gieseck, Heilemann and von Loeffelholz (1992) simulated positive employment effects in the context of a macroeconometric model.

Winkelmann and Zimmermann (1993) have examined the relationship between ageing, migration and labor mobility. Labor mobility is measured as the frequency of unemployment and by the number of direct job changes. They show that foreigners are more mobile than Germans. In younger age cohorts foreigners are less often unemployed than natives, but this changes drastically with age, and in older age cohorts foreigners are much more unemployed than natives. The share of foreigners in industries did not affect direct job changes of natives, but had a negative impact on the frequency of unempoyment of West Germans. De New and Zimmermann (1993) have studied the issue of substitutability by looking at the earnings of blue collar and white collar workers. They found foreigners to be substitutes to blue collar workers but complements to white collar workers.

This paper extends the framework of De New and Zimmermann (1993) by concentrating on blue collar workers. This group basically is the rival group for foreigners since immigrants in Germany are basically blue collar workers. Another group not studied by De New and Zimmermann (1993) is the group of immigrant workers themselves, who are expected to be strong substitutes to foreign workers themselves. Within the group of blue collar workers differences will be studied for experienced and unexperienced workers.

3 Data and Estimation Method

The data used is the West German Socio-Economic Panel (*Sozioökonomisches Panel*), which is provided by the *Deutsches Institut für Wirtschaftsforschung* (DIW) in Berlin. We were able to use variables from 6 waves (1984-1989). The data were retrieved from compressed Zoo (2.1) ASCII data files using Goetz Rohwer's RZoo (1.2) public domain program. In selecting the individual observations, we chose only employed blue collar males, both German and foreign, having a complete set of information for all relevant variables for at least 2 waves.

The final sample consists of 1153 employed German males and 1127 employed foreign males working in Germany from the six waves with a total number of observations of 4218 and 4320 respectively. For both the German and foreign group, those with 20 years of experience or more are compared with those having less, thereby making a total of 4 subgroups.

Following the theoretical framework, we use naturally logged hourly gross wages as the endogenous variable. As explanatory variables, the standard variables from the "earnings regression" approach have to be considered here. (See for instance Schmidt and Zimmermann (1991) for an outline of the variables used in this approach.) The most important are: EXPERIENCE defined as age - schooling - six, EXPERIENCE^2 and YEARS OF EDUCATION which measure human capital. A possible decay of human capital is proxied by the variable MONTHS UNEMPLOYED, the number of months the individual was previously unemployed during the last 10 years. Other variables were included to characterize the individual more closely: A dummy variable captures the marital status (MARRIED). The "low" job level blue collar variable (BLUE COLLAR LOW) captures the wage differences due to the qualication level, with the "high" job level blue collar workers being used as the dummy reference group. Further, the location is taken into account, i. e. whether the individual lives in a smaller city (CITY SMALL) of under 100,000, or a larger city (100,000 and over). The reference group in the regressions is "large city".

We also consider some foreigner-specific variables such as: length of stay (months) in quadratic form F-STAYLENGTH, the subjective ability to read and write German from 0 to 1, F-READGERMAN and F-WRITEGERMAN, and the following origin dummies: F-YUGOSLAVIAN, F-ITALIAN, F-SPANISH, with Turkish/Greek being the reference group.

Other variables to capture industry differences and work characteristics were included in the form of dummy variables. The following industry classifications were used: primary (I-PRIMAR), energy (I-ENERGY), investment (I-INVESTMENT), consumption (I-CONSUMPTION), construction (I-CONSTRUCTION), wholesale/retail (I-SELLING), transportation (I-TRANSPORT), banking (I-BANK) and restaurant/cleaning (I-REST/CLEAN). The omitted "reference group" is SERVICE-OTHER .

Several subjective job-characteristic dummy indicators are chosen to proxy possible reasons for additional wage compensation, and to describe the job in more detail: The variables are "bad job conditions" (J-BADCONDITION), "shift work" (J-SHIFTWORK), "hard work" (J-HARDWORK), and "possibility of on-the-job training" (J-JOBTRAIN). Further, it is often argued that larger firms pay higher wages for efficiency wage arguments. To account for this, we use a dummy indicator for firms with 200 and more employees (J-LARGEFIRM). In addition, on a general macro-level, the proportion of foreign workers (FOREIGNSHARE) has been calculated for each major industry classification in each year. Wages should respond positively to this share if natives are complements and negatively if they are substitutes. The average unemployment rate (UNEMPLOYMENT) for the appropriate German *Länder* and year is also taken into account. It is predicted that *Länder* wide unemployment rates negatively affect the wage. For those persons missing information on residence location, the German overall unemployment average is substituted. The industry-specific value-added growth (GROWTH) for each year is included to control for heterogeneous industry demand. A positive impact of sector growth on wages is expected. All of these macro data capture supply and demand effects not covered sufficiently by the industry dummies. These data are taken from the German Statistical Yearbook, using issues 1985 to 1992.

To estimate the wage function for each skill catagory, a random effects model is employed, with the individual-specific component in the error term:

(1) $\quad w_{it} = \alpha + \beta' X_{it} + \varepsilon_{it} + u_i,$

where

(2) $\quad u_i \sim N(0, \delta^2_u), \quad COV(\varepsilon_{it}, u_i) = 0.$

The model is estimated by 2-stage GLS using LIMDEP [6.0] (Greene, 1992) in the following manner: (a) the variance components are estimated using the residuals from OLS regressions and (b) GLS estimates are calculated using these estimated variances. Note that the wage functions are separately estimated for low and high qualified employees. A Lagrange multiplier test for the random effects model devised by Breusch and Pagan (1980) which is based on the OLS residuals and has $\chi^2(1)$ distribution can be used to examine whether the Panel GLS model is appropriate and the simple pooling has to be rejected.

The key hypothesis of the paper relates to the effect parameter of the share of foreign labor (FOREIGN SHARE). A problem here seems to be that the sector presence of foreigners may well be the result of high wages, and therefore, stem from reverse causation. Instrumentation would then be required. We have used the full sample as the basis for an OLS regression that explained Foreign Share by industry dummies, industry growth rates, an overall and industry specific time trend, which resulted in a R^2 of 0.45.

4 Empirical Results

Tables 1 through 3 contain the wage functions for the total sample, German blue collar and foreign blue collar labor, respectively, in which "one-way" random effects estimations are presented. For each German/foreign subsample and their respective further disaggregation into high/low experience, two estimations are presented. The first estimation contains all usual variables mentioned along with the industry foreigner share. The second estimation contains again all usual variables, but instead this time disaggregates the foreigner share by industry. The difference is basically the overall impact of foreigners averaged across all industries compared to the *industry-specific* impact. The overall impact might be negligible, but *industry-specific* positive effects might be cancelled out by another industry's negative effects. The tables also contain the Breusch-Pagan Lagrange Multiplier (LM) test. The LM statistics are overwhelmingly significant and support the appropriateness of the Panel GLS model specification in all cases.

Table 1 exhibits the wage functions of the total sample (German and foreign blue collar). The foreign share of labor has a negative impact. The usual empirical finding of an "inverted-U" shaped wage profile, consistent throughout all models, results from the positive and significant effect of experience and the negative and significant effect of experience-squared. Years of schooling have a significant and positive influence, adding to the human capital stock, whereas previous unemployment spells deplete the human capital stock. Those married, or living in larger cities, or working in larger firms perform better. Compared to low level blue collar workers, a premium is paid to high level workers. Industrial sectors have also consequences for wages. Comparing "SERVICE-OTHER", wage premiums are paid in the investment, primary, consumption, consruction, retail/wholoesale, and construction sectors on average.

Among the job characteristic variables, "hard work" effects are found to be significantly negative. This is contrary to the intuition that "hard work" would require positive compensation. Perhaps, as this is a subjective question, many see their jobs being as "hard work" or asking too much from them. The variable could therefore measure unobserved inabilities. The compensation hypothesis does receive support from jobs described as having "bad conditions", entering positively in the equation. "Wrong" signs of the coefficients of some job characteristic variables is a known phenomenon in the literature. (See Schmidt and Zimmermann (1991).)

From the macro-economic side, we examined the potential impact of industry-specific growth, regional (Länder-wide) unemployment and the share of foreign labor in the sectors. Regional unemployment has a significantly negative effect overall, as was expected, whereas the growth effect is positive but not significant at the 5% level.

The key variable in this study is the share of foreign labor in the industry sectors. A higher share should affect wages positively, if foreigners are complements and negatively, if they are substitutes. Here we see a significantly negative effect overall. The wage elasticity is simply the product of the estimated coefficient and its mean. In Column 1, using the coefficient on foreigner share, one can calculate the overall wage / foreigner share elasticity to be -0.65 i.e. a 1% increase in the share of foreigners has a 0.65% *decrease* in the hourly wage across the board. The average foreigner share is 10% across all industries. A 1%-*point* increase from 10.2% to 11.2% implies an increase of 9.8% in the foreigner share, further implying a 6.4% reduction in the hourly wage, translating to a DM 1.00 *reduction* for the average hourly wage of DM 15.51.

In Column 2 of Table 1, we see the industry-specific effects of the share of foreigners. For instance, large negative elasticities are found in the following industries: Primary (-0.64), Consumption (-0.24), Construction (-0.32). Small overall positive elasticities are obtained in: Transportation (+0.06) and Wholesale/Retail (+0.006). The message is that very few industries are gaining but most are losing on the average. It appears that foreigners are *on the whole* not only substitutes to native German blue collar workers but also to themselves. There is however the added threat of unemployment. Actually, Winkelmann and

Zimmermann (1992) were able to trace a larger frequency of German unemployment back to a larger share of foreign labor. Therefore, it seems to be that immigration affects not only wages but also employment opportunities. Since individual and economy-wide unemployment depreciates human capital significantly (see Table 1), there is an indirect effect of migrants on wages not covered in the discussion above.

Tables 2 and 3 report the results from the separately estimated panel regression for German and foreign blue collar workers respectively. From the original regression found in Table 1, it seems unnecessary to split the sample by nationality. Table 2 and 3 gives some persuasive reasons why this in fact is useful. Both tables further split each nationality group into high and low expereince levels. Here we have defined the high experience level to be 20 years or more.

Comparing the variable CITY SMALL for Germans and foreigners, we see very substantial negative effects for foreigners who work in smaller cities, compared to no significant effect for Germans. With often few qualifications, foreigners traditionally move to the more diverse labor marktets of larger cities. Those who stay in smaller cities, are penalized.

When looking at human capital erosion due to personal unemployment MONTHS UNEMPLOY, there are are also some surprising results. For equal lengths of unemployment spells, foreigners suffer approximately twice as much human capital erosion as their German counterparts, as indicated by lower wages. Unemployment at the national level affects foreigners' wages only slightly more, or equally negatively than those of Germans as demonstrated by the variable UNEMPLOYMENT. However it is also interesting to note that in times of growth, the wage gains from growth are disproportionally shared. High experienced Germans gain almost twice as much due to growth than their equivalent foreign counterparts.

Language skills (Table 3, column 5 and 6) for foreigners seem not be very important on the whole. For those low experienced foreign blue collar workers, the greater the ability to speak German, the higher the wage is perhaps not so surprising. As workers often engage in physical activity, it is not surprising that the ability to write German well has no advantage. As not all foreigners are not *de facto* the same, originating country dummies were used. Using TURKISH/GREEK as the reference group, there is no advantage being from one country or another, expect for a strong negative effect coming from ITALIAN.

Turning now to the variable FOREIGN SHARE, the industry specific proportion of foreigners, one observes a similar inequality. High experienced Germans seem not to have their wages significantly affected by foreigners in their industries. On the other hand, Germans with less than 20 years experience are significantly negatively affected. The large coefficient size reiterates the importance of this variable in the earnings equation. Again, foreign blue collar workers with 20 or more years of experience are disproportionately negatively affected by almost twice as much. Concretely, to illustrate the magnitude of these effects, we simulate a 1%-point increase from the mean in the foreigner share, translating to a 10.2% and 9.8% increase for Germans and foreigners respectively. Then using the elasticity calculated from the product of the variable's mean and coefficient, the wage effect can be quantified. Looking at the impact of increased foreigner share, averaged across all industries, we find the following: For Germans with less than 20 years experience, having an elasticity of -0.213, this translates to a loss of DM 0.32 (2.2%) per hour. However, highly experienced foreign workers, having an elasticitiy of -0.412, experience a loss of DM 0.63 (4.0%) per hour, a significantly higher proportion. One must conclude that established foreign workers are significantly negatively affected by new arrivals working in their industries, far more so than their German counterparts, regardless of their experience level. Germans with more than 20 years of experience, along with foreigners with less than 20 years experience, are not significantly affected by increased foreigner share.

5 Conclusions

Examining the wage functions of blue collar natives and immigrants in a random effects panel model, we have studied the effect of immigration, measured by the share of foreigners in the industry branch, in which the employee works. We find that immigration appears to have an overall negative effect on native and immigrant blue-collar wages with some job groups and industries being hit harder than others. In this sense, foreigners must be seen as being overwhelmingly substitutes, depressing blue collar wages, native and immigrant alike. Disaggregating the native and immigrant blue collar groups by years of experience better illustrates the interaction of the gains and losses of specific groups as compared to others. Native workers with 20 years of experience or more seem as a group not to be affected significantly by increased migration. However, low experienced native workers do indeed suffer substantial downward wage pressure from increased migration. High-experienced immigrant workers suffer even more from increased migration, bearing the brunt of the large negative migration effect with particularly strong negative effects found in the primary and construction industries. Low-experienced foreign workers seem not to be statistically affected by new migrants.

On average, for all blue collar workers, native and immigrant alike, a 1%-point increase in the foreigner share, implies a 6.4% reduction in the hourly wage. High experienced immigrant workers bear approximately twice as much of the wage reduction with 4.0% compared to low experienced German labor with 2.2%. This downward wage pressure documents the substitutability of new immigrant blue collar workers with less experienced German and more experienced immigrant blue collar labor. These findings are large in comparison to a recent study by Altonji and Card (1991) who found that the weekly earnings of less-skilled U.S. natives (including Afro-American and female workers) are reduced by about 1.2%. Nevertheless, the estimated effects for Germans are not considered to be dramatic in size.

Appendix

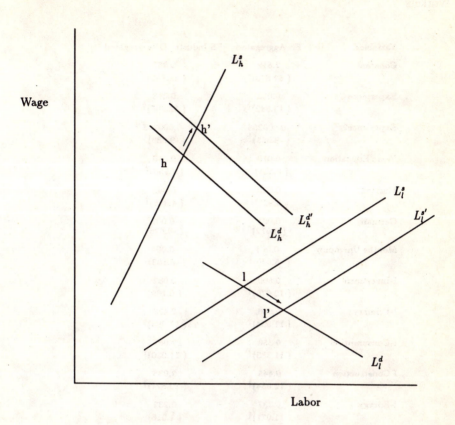

Figure 1: Labor Market Effects of Increased Immigration

Table 1: Wage Impacts of Migration on German and Foreign Blue Collar Workers

Variables	FS Aggregated	FS Industry Disaggregated
Constant	2.612 (52.813)†	2.262 (49.742)†
Experience	0.020 (13.542)†	0.018 (12.205)†
Experience2	-0.000296 (-9.985)†	-0.000283 (-9.633)†
Years Education	0.019 (8.531)†	0.016 (7.256)†
Married	0.039 (3.921)†	0.042 (4.305)†
German	0.001 (0.072)	-0.007 (-0.626)
Months Unemploy	-0.004 (-5.440)†	-0.004 (-6.183)†
I-Investment	0.509 (12.676)†	0.082 (0.169)
I-Primary	0.656 (11.934)†	2.438 (17.095)†
I-Consumption	0.358 (11.383)†	2.087 (11.030)†
I-Construction	0.445 (12.034)†	2.036 (10.624)†
I-Energy	0.337 (11.071)†	0.232 (1.016)
I-Selling	0.085 (4.050)†	-0.045 (-0.769)
I-Transport	0.166 (7.005)†	-0.829 (-2.070)†
I-Banking	-0.142 (-1.763)‡	0.421 (1.495)
I-Rest/Cleaning	0.371 (7.743)†	1.355 (6.008)†
Blue Collar Low	-0.046 (-8.208)†	-0.045 (-8.258)†
J-LargeFirm	0.067 (9.398)†	0.063 (8.885)†
J-BadCondtion	0.019 (3.352)†	0.014 (2.560)†
J-JobTraining	0.006 (1.186)	0.007 (1.488)

Table 1, continued

Variables	FS Aggregated	FS Industry Disaggregated
J-HardWork	-0.022	-0.019
	(-3.863)†	(-3.530)†
J-ShiftWork	0.032	0.026
	(4.887)†	(4.050)†
City Small	-0.054	-0.052
	(-6.351)†	(-6.133)†
Growth	0.044	-0.101
	(1.103)	(-2.228)†
Unemployment	-0.019	-0.015
	(-12.203)†	(-9.437)†
ForeignShare	-6.374	–
	(-9.940)†	
FS-Investment	–	1.526
		(0.332)
FS-Primary	–	-16.943
		(-15.978)†
FS-Consumption	–	-21.049
		(-10.238)†
FS-Construction	–	-18.189
		(-9.711)†
FS-Energy	–	0.469
		(0.152)
FS-Selling	–	3.614
		(4.048)†
FS-Transport	–	13.885
		(2.408)†
FS-Bank	–	-15.873
		(-0.890)
FS-Rest/Cleaning	–	-11.625
		(-5.827)†
FS-Service Other	–	2.403
		(3.398)†
N	8752	8752
R^2	0.195	0.225
$LM(d.f.=1)$	2359.956	2478.660
σ_e^2	0.029	0.028
σ_u^2	0.028	0.027

† t-values in parentheses - significant at 5% level ‡ t-values in parentheses - significant at 5% level - one tail test

Table 2: Wage Effects of Migration on German Blue Collar Workers

Variables	Total	Total	High Experience	High Experience	Low Experience	Low Experience
Constant	2.325 (37.045)†	2.273 (35.582)†	2.551 (16.997)†	2.369 (15.763)†	2.063 (21.929)†	2.099 (21.991)†
Experience	0.019 (9.144)†	0.017 (8.438)†	0.000472 (0.057)	0.0082 (1.026)	0.045 (6.959)†	0.038 (5.829)†
Experience2	-0.000275 (-6.483)†	-0.000264 (-6.306)†	0.000054 (0.413)	-0.000108 (-0.839)	-0.00118 (-4.419)†	-0.0010 (-3.741)†
Years Education	0.024 (7.052)†	0.022 (6.547)†	0.020 (4.003)†	0.017 (3.449)†	0.033 (7.431)†	0.031 (6.870)†
Married	0.038 (3.509)†	0.037 (3.516)†	0.019 (1.016)	0.021 (1.184)	0.042 (3.116)†	0.044 (3.285)†
Months Unemployed	-0.003 (-3.219)†	-0.003 (-3.844)†	-0.003 (-2.522)†	-0.003 (-2.815)†	-0.004 (-3.017)†	-0.004 (-3.251)†
I-Investment	0.222 (8.434)†	-0.708 (-0.920)	0.197 (4.781)†	0.915 (0.857)	0.218 (6.417)†	-2.308 (-2.103)†
I-Primary	0.266 (7.608)†	2.294 (10.757)†	0.216 (3.929)†	2.268 (7.865)†	0.281 (6.299)†	1.827 (5.429)†
I-Consumption	0.147 (6.473)†	2.680 (9.664)†	0.122 (3.495)†	2.721 (6.743)†	0.147 (5.012)†	2.259 (5.640)†
I-Construction	0.177 (7.030)†	1.904 (6.920)†	0.149 (3.903)†	2.151 (6.006)†	0.193 (5.860)†	1.070 (2.349)†
I-Energy	0.195 (5.933)†	0.179 (0.538)	0.228 (4.937)†	0.531 (1.234)	0.150 (3.364)†	-0.254 (-0.482)
I-Selling	0.032 (1.237)	-0.154 (-2.010)†	0.036 (0.932)	-0.173 (-1.500)	0.007 (0.209)	-0.120 (-1.156)
I-Transport	0.052 (2.374)†	-0.978 (-1.951)‡	0.073 (2.492)†	-1.568 (-2.495)†	-0.004 (-0.120)	0.511 (0.595)
Blue Collar Low	-0.063 (-7.633)†	-0.063 (-7.850)†	-0.059 (-5.372)†	-0.060 (-5.593)†	-0.069 (-5.642)†	-0.068 (-5.639)†
J-LargeFirm	0.074 (7.256)†	0.074 (7.405)†	0.058 (4.032)†	0.061 (4.325)†	0.092 (6.606)†	0.091 (6.569)†
J-BadConditions	0.020 (2.270)†	0.017 (2.007)†	0.015 (1.311)	0.014 (1.223)	0.021 (1.623)	0.019 (1.490)
J-JobTraining	-0.006 (-0.799)	-0.006 (-0.869)	-0.004 (-0.390)	-0.003 (-0.292)	-0.011 (-0.962)	-0.013 (-1.188)
J-HardWork	-0.024 (-2.816)†	-0.026 (-3.044)†	-0.023 (-2.042)†	-0.024 (-2.197)†	-0.014 (-1.092)	-0.017 (-1.348)
J-ShiftWork	0.048 (4.879)†	0.039 (4.016)†	0.059 (4.184)†	0.047 (3.388)†	0.031 (2.246)†	0.025 (1.873)‡
City Small	-0.050 (-4.536)†	-0.046 (-4.166)†	-0.077 (-4.971)†	-0.071 (-4.644)†	-0.016 (-1.036)	-0.014 (-0.943)

Table 2, continued

Variables	Total	Total	High Experience	High Experience	Low Experience	Low Experience
Growth	0.143 (2.712)†	-0.143 (-2.207)†	0.213 (2.972)†	-0.118 (-1.310)	0.029 (0.374)	-0.141 (-1.473)
Unemployment	-0.017 (-7.490)†	-0.011 (-5.124)†	-0.016 (-5.241)†	-0.010 (-3.429)†	-0.013 (-3.925)†	-0.010 (-3.055)†
Foreign Share	-1.610 (-3.571)†	—	-0.806 (-1.154)	—	-2.166 (-3.680)†	—
FS-Investment	—	7.986 (1.093)	—	-6.617 (-0.653)	—	22.262 (2.135)†
FS-Primary	—	-16.569 (-10.272)†	—	-15.757 (-7.240)†	—	-13.672 (-5.368)†
FS-Consumption	—	-28.779 (-9.487)†	—	-28.454 (-6.438)†	—	-25.000 (-5.702)†
FS-Construction	—	-18.053 (-6.663)†	—	-19.792 (-5.615)†	—	-10.500 (-2.340)†
FS-Energy	—	-0.451 (-0.099)	—	-3.774 (-0.647)	—	3.975 (0.544)
FS-Selling	—	3.249 (2.603)†	—	4.948 (2.714)†	—	0.939 (0.548)
FS-Transport	—	14.431 (1.997)†	—	24.407 (2.697)†	—	-8.954 (-0.722)
FS-Service Other	—	-0.450 (-0.901)	—	0.867 (1.091)	—	-1.569 (-2.460)†
N	4218	4218	2342	2342	1876	1876
R^2	0.236	0.268	0.162	0.206	0.293	0.317
$LM(d.f.=1)$	1054.746	1141.508	687.831	749.526	286.116	292.229
σ_e^2	0.029	0.027	0.027	0.026	0.029	0.028
σ_u^2	0.025	0.024	0.028	0.026	0.022	0.022

† t-values in parentheses - significant at 5% level ‡ t-values in parentheses - significant at 5% level - one tail test

Table 3: Wage Effects of Migration on Foreign Blue Collar Workers

Variables	Total	Total	High Experience	High Experience	Low Experience	Low Experience
Constant	2.395 (35.773)†	2.410 (34.468)†	2.796 (22.791)†	2.803 (22.656)†	1.923 (14.768)†	1.978 (14.217)†
Experience	0.015 (6.390)†	0.015 (6.515)†	-0.007 (-1.042)	-0.007 (-1.020)	0.060 (7.076)†	0.052 (6.074)†
Experience2	-0.000277 (-6.405)†	-0.000285 (-6.630)†	0.000060 (0.591)	0.000053 (0.523)	-0.00200 (-4.532)†	-0.00100 (-4.005)†
Years Education	0.008 (2.596)†	0.006 (2.050)†	0.003 (0.990)	0.003 (0.842)	0.016 (3.147)†	0.013 (2.538)†
Married	-0.003 (-0.065)	0.028 (0.706)	-0.055 (-0.848)	-0.023 (-0.351)	0.011 (0.220)	0.037 (0.710)
Months Unemploy	-0.004 (-4.134)†	-0.004 (-4.484)†	-0.006 (-5.083)†	-0.006 (-5.277)†	-0.002 (-1.166)	-0.002 (-1.374)
I-Investment	0.216 (7.848)†	0.257 (0.404)	0.305 (7.950)†	-0.528 (-0.654)	0.122 (2.937)†	1.207 (1.059)
I-Primary	0.255 (7.062)†	1.857 (9.383)†	0.383 (7.427)†	1.491 (6.098)†	0.138 (2.628)†	2.177 (5.229)†
I-Consumption	0.135 (5.364)†	0.950 (3.499)†	0.188 (5.601)†	0.442 (1.201)	0.098 (2.472)†	1.338 (2.898)†
I-Construction	0.183 (6.768)†	1.486 (5.257)†	0.272 (7.397)†	1.308 (3.759)†	0.131 (3.148)†	0.900 (1.525)
I-Energy	0.203 (5.048)†	0.218 (0.666)	0.207 (4.534)†	-0.202 (-0.500)	0.277 (3.814)†	0.760 (1.182)
I-Selling	0.026 (0.785)	-0.230 (-2.592)†	0.146 (3.426)†	-0.089 (-0.648)	-0.059 (-1.004)	-0.213 (-1.556)
I-Transport	0.010 (0.339)	-0.741 (-1.089)	0.034 (0.988)	-1.426 (-1.812)‡	-0.035 (-0.583)	3.411 (2.036)†
Blue Collar Low	-0.023 (-3.040)†	-0.024 (-3.151)†	-0.027 (-2.861)†	-0.027 (-2.949)†	-0.012 (-0.883)	-0.012 (-0.861)
J-LargeFirm	0.059 (5.908)†	0.059 (5.910)†	0.053 (4.495)†	0.053 (4.532)†	0.087 (4.870)†	0.087 (4.953)†
J-BadConditions	0.008 (1.105)	0.006 (0.802)	0.010 (1.118)	0.010 (1.038)	0.010 (0.804)	0.009 (0.700)
J-JobTraining	0.012 (1.762)‡	0.015 (2.237)†	0.010 (1.197)	0.013 (1.594)	0.025 (2.031)†	0.023 (1.882)‡
J-HardWork	-0.009 (-1.247)	-0.007 (-0.990)	-0.006 (-0.676)	-0.005 (-0.521)	-0.014 (-1.126)	-0.008 (-0.658)
J-Shiftwork	0.025 (2.932)†	0.020 (2.365)†	0.014 (1.348)	0.011 (1.047)	0.051 (3.310)†	0.045 (2.954)†
City Small	-0.062 (-4.821)†	-0.061 (-4.755)†	-0.046 (-3.228)†	-0.047 (-3.331)†	-0.079 (-3.416)†	-0.073 (-3.127)†

Table 3, continued

Variables	Total	Total	High Experience	High Experience	Low Experience	Low Experience
F-StayLength	0.020 (11.352)†	0.015 (8.204)†	0.022 (9.945)†	0.018 (7.769)†	0.013 (3.886)†	0.010 (3.060)†
F-StayLength2	-0.000191 (-10.419)†	-0.000143 (-7.550)†	-0.000201 (-9.222)†	-0.000164 (-7.253)†	-0.000120 (-3.464)†	-0.000095 (-2.725)†
F-WriteGerman	0.002 (0.142)	0.003 (0.162)	0.009 (0.464)	0.012 (0.591)	-0.003 (-0.112)	-0.007 (-0.217)
F-TalkGerman	0.024 (1.254)	0.025 (1.310)	0.008 (0.321)	0.009 (0.394)	0.086 (2.328)†	0.088 (2.437)†
F-Yugoslavian	0.025 (1.581)	0.024 (1.485)	0.021 (1.251)	0.015 (0.930)	0.013 (0.391)	0.033 (0.949)
F-Italian	-0.011 (-0.732)	-0.009 (-0.600)	-0.038 (-2.133)†	-0.033 (-1.864)‡	-0.001 (-0.047)	0.002 (0.062)
F-Spanish	-0.011 (-0.635)	-0.005 (-0.272)	-0.012 (-0.615)	-0.007 (-0.394)	-0.023 (-0.647)	-0.009 (-0.252)
Growth	0.152 (3.033)†	-0.057 (-0.871)	0.118 (1.900)‡	0.025 (0.309)	0.175 (1.847)‡	-0.092 (-0.773)
Unemployment	-0.019 (-8.691)†	-0.016 (-7.340)†	-0.016 (-6.775)†	-0.015 (-6.252)†	-0.018 (-4.170)†	-0.015 (-3.551)†
Foreign Share	-2.401 (-4.825)†	–	-3.898 (-5.839)†	–	-1.071 (-1.264)	–
A-Investment	–	-2.162 (-0.358)	–	4.542 (0.594)	–	-10.701 (-0.994)
A-Primary	–	-14.192 (-9.615)†	–	-11.971 (-6.563)†	–	-16.105 (-5.214)†
A-Construction	–	-14.754 (-5.322)†	–	-13.656 (-4.001)†	–	-8.118 (-1.408)
A-Consumption	–	-10.811 (-3.664)†	–	-6.170 (-1.537)	–	-14.088 (-2.820)†
A-Energy	–	-2.005 (-0.457)	–	2.262 (0.416)	–	-7.144 (-0.826)
A-Selling	–	3.542 (2.580)†	–	1.127 (0.523)	–	3.233 (1.675)‡
A-Transport	–	9.414 (0.959)	–	18.009 (1.588)	–	-49.941 (-2.058)†
A-Service Other	–	-1.585 (-2.747)†	–	-3.070 (-3.981)†	–	-0.474 (-0.483)
N	4320	4320	3111	3111	1209	1209
R^2	0.180	0.205	0.174	0.193	0.237	0.254
$LM(d.f.=1)$	1067.611	1110.437	785.519	785.434	215.752	230.543
σ_e^2	0.029	0.028	0.028	0.028	0.030	0.030
σ_u^2	0.029	0.027	0.022	0.022	0.035	0.036

† t-values in parentheses - significant at 5% level ‡ t-values in parentheses - significant at 5% level - one tail test

References

Altonji, J.G. and D. Card (1991): "The Effects of Immigration on the Labor Market Outcomes of Less-Skilled Natives." in J.M. Abowd and R.B. Freeman (eds.), <u>Immigration, Trade, and the Labor Market,</u> 201-234. Chicago: University of Chicago Press

Akbari, A.H. and D.J. Devoretz (1992): "The Substitutability of Foreign Born in Canadian Production: Circa 1980", <u>Canadian Journal of Economics</u>, 25,3, 604-614.

Barbaras, G. and A. Gieseck, U. Heilemann and H.D. von Loeffelholz (1992): "Gesamtwirtschaftliche Effekte der Zuwanderung", <u>RWI-Mitteilungen</u>, 43, 133-154.

Bean F.D., B. Lindsay Lowell and L.J. Taylor (1988): "Undocumented Mexican Immigrants and Earnings of Other Workers in the United States", <u>Demography</u>, 25, 35-49.

Borjas, G.J. (1983): "The Substituability of Black, Hispanic and White Labor", <u>Economic Inquiry</u>, 21, 93-106.

Borjas, G.J. (1986): "Immigrants in the U.S. Labor Market" in S. Pozo (Ed.)<u>Essays on Legal and Illegal Immigration,</u> Washington, D.C.: W.E. Upjohn Institute for Employment Research, 7-20.

Borjas, G.J., R.B. Freeman and L.F. Katz (1991): "<u>On the Labor Market Effects of Immigration and Trade</u>", NBER Working Paper, No. 3761. Cambridge, Mass.

Breusch, T. and A. Pagan (1980): "The LM Test and its Application to Model Specification in Econometrics", <u>Review of Econometric Studies</u> 47, 239-254.

Davila, A. and P.J. Mattila (1985): "Do Workers Earn Less Along the Texas-Mexican Border ?", <u>Social Science Quarterly,</u> 66, 310-318.

DeFreitas, G. and A. Marshall (1983): "Immigration and Wage Growth in U.S. Manufacturing in the 1970's", Paper presented at the <u>AEA/IRRA Meetings</u>, San Francisco, California.

De New, J.P. and K.F. Zimmermann (1993): "<u>Native Wage Impacts of Foreign Labor: A Random Effects Panel Analysis</u>", forthcoming Journal of Population Economics, London.

German Statistical Office <u>German Statistical Yearbook</u>, 1985-1992.

Greene, W. (1992): "<u>LIMDEP [6.0] User's Manual and Reference Guide</u>", Econometric Software, Bellport, NY.

Greenwood, M.J. and J.M. McDowell (1986): "The Factor Market Consequences of U.S. Immigration", <u>Journal of Economic Literature,</u> 24, 1738-1772.

Hamermesh, D.S. (1986): "The Demand for Labour in the Long Run", in: O.C. Ashenfelter and R. Layard (eds.) <u>Handbook of Labour Economics</u>, Vol.1 Amsterdam: North-Holland, 429-471.

Heckman, J.J. and G. Sedlacek (1985): "Heterogeneity, Aggregation, and Market Wage Functions: An Empirical Model of Self-selection in the Labour Market", Journal of Political Economy 93, 1077-1125.

LaLonde R.J. and R.H. Topel (1991): "Immigrants in the American Labor Market: Quality, Assimilation and Distributional Effects", American Economic Review 81, (P&P), 291-302.

Matta, B. and A. Popp (1985): "Immigration and the Earnings of Youth in the United States", International Migration Review, 22, 104-116.

Rivera-Batiz, F.L. and S.L. Sechzer (1991): "Substitution and Complementarity between Immigrant and Native Labour in the United States" in F.L. Rivera-Batiz, S.L. Sechzer and I.N. Gang (eds.) U.S. Immigration Policy Reform in the 1980's, New York, Praeger, 1991, 89-116.

Rohwer, G. (1992a): "A Retrieval Program for the SOEP", EMPAS-University of Bremen, mimeo.

Rohwer, G. (1992b): "RZoo: Efficient Storage and Retrieval of Social Science Data", EUI Working Paper No. 92/19, Florence.

Schmidt, C.M. and K.F. Zimmermann (1991): "Work Characteristics, Firm Size and Wages", Review of Economics and Statistics 73, 705-710.

Schmidt, C.M. and K.F. Zimmermann (1992): "Migration Pressure in Germany: Past and Future", in K.F. Zimmermann (ed.) Migration and Economic Development. Springer: New York, 201-230.

Spitznagel, E. (1987): "Gesamtwitschaftliche Aspekte der Ausländerbeschäftigung", Beiträge zur Arbeitsmarkt- und Berufsforschung, 114, 243-286.

Smith, B. and R. Newman (1977): "Depressed Wages Along the U.S.-Mexican Border: An Empirical Analysis", Economic Inquiry, 82, 34-55.

Straubhaar, T. and K.F. Zimmermann (1992): "Towards a European Migration Policy", CEPR Discussion Paper No. 641, forthcoming: Population Research and Policy Review.

Taylor, L.J., F.D. Bean, J.B. Rebitzer, S. Gonzalez-Baker and B.L. Lowell (1988): "Mexican Immigrants and the Wages and Unemployment Experience of Native Workers", Working Paper PRIP-UI-1, The Urban Institute.

Wehrmann, M. (1989): "Auswirkungen der Ausländerbeschäftigung auf die Volkswirtschaft der Bundesrepublik Deutschland in Vergangenheit und Zukunft", Baden-Baden: Nomos.

Winegarden, C.R. and L.B. Khor (1993): "Undocumented Immigration and Income Inequality in the Native-Born Population of the US: Econometric Evidence", Applied Economics, 25, 157-163.

Winkelmann, R. and K.F. Zimmermann (1993): "Ageing, Migration and Labor Mobility, in: D. Johnson and K.F. Zimmermann (Eds.), Labour Markets in an Ageing Europe, Cambridge University Press, 255-283.

Re-Migration Behavior and Expected Duration of Stay of Guest Workers in Germany

Viktor Steiner
Zentrum für Europäische Wirtschaftsforschung (ZEW)
Kaiserring 14-16
68161 Mannheim, Germany

Johannes Velling
Zentrum für Europäische Wirtschaftsforschung (ZEW)
Kaiserring 14-16
68161 Mannheim, Germany

1 Introduction

Compared to other immigration countries, the German guest worker system is peculiar in various respects. The great majority of guest workers migrated to Germany from Turkey, (the former) Yugoslavia, Italy, Greece and Spain in the late sixties and early seventies, when the federal labor office was actively hiring guest workers through recruitment treaties. At that time it was expected, both by the German authorities and by the guest workers themselves, that the workers would stay only temporarily in Germany. The dominating factor for temporary migration was believed to be the so-called "savings motive", implying that guest workers would return to their home countries after they had saved enough money either to set up a small private business or to live in retirement back home. However, a considerable number of them became permanent residents, either because economic and/or political developments in the source countries rendered return migration unattractive, or simply because of successful integration in German society. Although expected duration of stay varies among individuals, guest workers have similar earnings/experience profiles as natives. This can be interpreted as strong evidence for their successful integration into the German labor market (Licht/Steiner, 1992).

There are only a few theoretical studies which address the issue of return migration in a guest worker system from the perspective of the migrant worker. In the model of Djajic/Milbourne (1988), an individual's migration decision, as well as the rate of saving while abroad and the optimal length of a migrant's stay in the host country, are derived as solutions to an intertemporal optimization problem. In their model, optimal length of stay is determined by the wage differential between the host and home countries and by the costs of migration. Ceteris paribus, it depends negatively on the wage in the home country and positively on the costs of migration. The qualitative effect of a wage increase in the host country depends on the migrant's relative degree risk aversion. For very risk averse individuals, the optimal length of stay decreases with a wage increase in the host country. Dustmann (1992) adds to this model the important point that changes in the optimal length of stay in the host country may also be affected by an "environmental factor", assumed to be complementary to consumption. This factor in turn, is assumed to be affected by the migrant's social integration in the host country. As a migrant becomes more integrated in the host country, the optimal duration of stay may change and may eventually become permanent.

There are some studies on guest workers' expectations or realisations of return migration in Germany which are based on survey data. For Turkish guest workers, Werth (1983) found that only a minority planned to stay permanently in Germany. For those who planned to re-migrate, the important factors influencing their decision to return were: age and duration of stay in Germany, marital status, the level of earnings and an individual's labor market status (unemployment). Münzenmaier/Walter (1983) found, inter alia, that the proportion of guest workers intending to stay permanently increases with the time elapsed since their arrival in Germany. They also observed considerable differences in intended duration of stay between the various nationalities. Brecht (1990) analyzed the re-migration behavior of Turkish guest workers in Germany and found that older workers have a higher return probability. Although these studies shed some light on important determinants of individual re-migration decisions, they do not attempt to isolate the various factors and, therefore remain somewhat agnostic on their relative importance. Based on a sample of Turkish guest workers, Hönekopp (1987) analyzed the determinants of re-migration behavior and the effects of the "return promotion act" of 1983 in particular.

A more quantitative approach is pursued in the study by Dustmann (1992), which is based on an econometric model of return migration estimated on a single cross-section of guest workers in Germany. In this study, individual re-migration decisions are differentiated according to whether or not a guest worker intends to stay permanently in the host country. For temporary residents re-migration decisions are differentiated, according to expected duration of stay. It turns out that the determinants of both decisions are qualitatively rather similar. According to this study, important determinants of a guest worker's expected duration of stay in Germany are: age, the existence of a spouse living in the home country, number of years since migration, individual earnings and the individual's employment status at the date of interview. The estimated effects of these variables are, more or less, in accordance with the qualitative implications of the model.

In this paper, we attempt to extend existing empirical work on re-migration behavior to guest workers in Germany, where we focus on an individual's expected duration of stay. Given that the factors determining re-migration behavior remain constant, this variable should be a good predictor of an individual's actual re-migration decision and should thus contribute to an understanding of the determinants of observed re-migration, which seems important for the implementation of an effective migration policy. To this end, we include several important variables missing in the Dustmann study to account for the effect of social integration in German society on individual re-migration behavior. The observation period covers the years 1984 to 1989, for which we have panel data for guest workers available. So far, there seem to have been no related studies based on panel data for Germany or for any other country as well. An important advantage of the use of panel data is that more efficient parameter estimates can be obtained than were in previous studies based on cross-section data. Our approach also differs in the chosen statistical model, which seems more appropriate given the data at hand.

In the next section we give a brief description of our data base and define the variables used in the study. Section 3 describes the econometric model in some detail. Section 4 presents and discusses the estimation results, and the final section contains a summary and a conclusion.

2 Data and Variables Description

The empirical analysis is based on the first six waves of the Socio-Economic Panel (SOEP) for West Germany. In the first wave, some 12,000 individuals belonging to about 6,000 households were interviewed to determine a large number of personal and household characteristics as well as education, training and labor market experience (for a description of the SOEP see Wagner/Schupp/Rendtel, 1991). Foreigners from the main source countries for guest workers, i.e. Turkey, Yugoslavia, Italy, Greece and Spain, have deliberately been oversampled in the SOEP. This provides a unique opportunity to analyse the return migration decision of citizens from these countries in some detail.

The analysis is restricted to household heads, either male or female, because the assumption that family re-migration decisions are made by them seems plausible. The variable we want to explain is an individual's *expected duration of stay* in Germany at the date of interview in each wave. In the SOEP, guest workers are asked whether they intend to stay temporarily or permanently, where for temporary stayers their expected duration of stay is also recorded. Although this variable is recorded in years, we prefer to split it up into intervals, because responses to this question are heavily bunched at certain years, thus contaminating this variable with large measurement errors. As expected, not all guest workers had an opinion on their expected duration of stay, and were, therefore, excluded from the analysis (in the first wave, for example about 11 percent did not respond).

For temporary residents (at the date of the first interview, i.e. in 1984), Figure 1 shows strong ties at one, three, five, ten, fifteen etc. years, which suggests that the expected duration should be split up into several catagories.

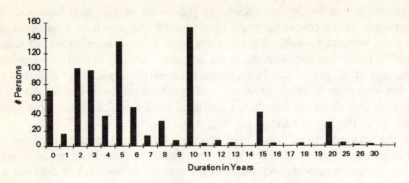

Figure 1. Expected Duration of Stay of Household Heads in 1984

Source: German Socio-Economic Panel, wave 1,: own calculations.

Our choice of categories was guided by two considerations: first, to have a sufficient number of observations falling within each time interval and second, to account for expected behavioral differences within each category. Thus, we distinguish between the following duration categories:

- *short-term*   (0 - 3 years),
- *mid-term*   (4 - 7 years),
- *long-term*   (8 - 30 years), and
- *permanent*.

Note that this catagorization also allows us to analyze re-migration behavior for both temporary and permanent migrants using the statistical model described in the next section[1]. The distribution of the observations in each wave within the observations period 1984 - 1989 is given in Table 1.

---

[1] Restricting the analysis to temporary residents and correcting for the resulting potential selectivity-bias with respect to the decision to stay permanently, does not seem a feasible alternative, as both decisions depend on the same variables. Identification could, therefore, only be achieved by functional form, i.e. the non-linearity of the selectivity-correction term, which seems to be a problematic approach (see, e.g., Rendtel, 1992).

Table 1: Distribution of Expected Duration of Stay of Guest workers, 1984 - 1989

Duration	1984	1985	1986	1987	1988	1989	1984 - 89
Short-term	25	20	20	18	14	13	19
Medium-term	19	22	22	21	19	15	20
Long-term	24	28	28	28	30	31	28
Permanent	31	30	30	33	37	40	33
$\sum$	1098	872	786	741	667	504	4668

Note: Numbers are percentages; due to rounding errors column sums may differ from 100. The last line gives the number of individuals in each wave; this number declines over the observation period due to both return migration and other forms of sample attrittion (non-response).

The table shows that the distribution of expected duration of stay has shifted to the long-term and permanent categories over the observation period. This may have resulted, either from a change in the composition of foreigners due to return-migration from changes in expectations due to the lenghtening of an individual's actual duration of stay, or from changes in other factors which determine return-migration. Re-migration behavior in 1984 was affected by the "return-promotion act" of 1983 which ruled that claimants of benefits paid for early re-migration had to leave Germany by September 1984 (see Hönekopp, 1987). This could explain the relatively high proportion of guest workers falling into the short-term category in that year.

Following the literature on return-migration referred to in the introduction, we include the following groups of variables as potential determinants of an immigrant's expected duration of stay in the model:

- *Personal characteristics*: sex, age, nationality, education, marital status, children in different age groups, disability;
- *Assimilation indicators*: years since migration, second generation dummy, children abroad, spouse abroad, language, subjective evaluation of well-being in Germany, owner of apartment/house;
- *Transfers*: yearly amount of transfers to home country, differentiated by kind of transfers;
- *Income variables*: labor earnings of household head, other net household income;
- *Labor Market Situation*: unemployment of household head and spouse; household head's cumulative unemployment within the last year.

Definitions of variables and summary statistics are contained in Table 2, where variables refer to mean values within the observation period 1984 - 1989. To make efficient use of the information in the sample, we work with an unbalanced panel design of the first six waves of the SOEP. Thus, individuals are included in the sample with the number of observations for an individual corresponding to the waves, in which he or she has taken part in the panel.

Table 2: Definition of Variables and Summary Statistics

Variable	Variable Definition	Mean / Proportion	Standard deviation
	Dependent Variable		
ESTAY_ST	Expected duration of stay in Germany = short term	19.0	-.-
ESTAY_MT	= medium term	20.1	-.-
ESTAY_LT	= long term	27.9	-.-
ESTAY_PT	= permanent	33.0	-.-
	Personal characteristics		
SEX	Female = 1	8.6	-.-
AGE	Years of age	42.9	9.8
AGE50	Years of age above 50 years = 1	24.0	-.-
NATY	Nationality = Yugoslavia	23.3	-.-
NATG	= Greece	13.4	-.-
NATI	= Italy	21.7	-.-
NATS	= Spain (base category = Turkey)	12.3	-.-
EDUC_LOW	Low education	30.0	-.-
EDUC_HIGH	High education (base category = no degree)	13.0	-.-
MARRIED	Married = 1	84.2	-.-
CHILD_5	Child up to 5 y. in household present = 1	25.5	-.-
CHILD_15	Child between 6 and 15 years = 1	46.4	-.-
CHILD_18	Child between 16 and 18 years = 1	19.2	-.-
CHILD_19	Child older than 18 years present = 1	24.0	-.-
DISABLED	Disabled = 1	5.8	-.-
	Integration indicators		
YSM	Years since migration to Germany	17.2	5.4
SECGEN	Belonging to second generation = 1	1.7	-.-
SPOUSE_A	Spouse living in home country = 1	6.1	-.-
CHILD_A	Children living in home country = 1	12.7	-.-
SPEAK_B	Knowledge of mother tongue = poor	0.9	-.-
SPEAK_G	= good; (base category = sufficient)	95.1	-.-
GSPEAK_B	Knowlege of spoken German = poor	17.3	-.-
GSPEAK_G	= good; (base category = sufficient)	44.0	-.-
FEEL_B	Subjective evaluation of well-being in Germany = bad	5.5	-.-
FEEL_G	= good (base category = indifferent)	68.2	-.-
OWNER	Owner of a house/apartment in Germany	6.5	-.-
	Transfers		

Table 2 continued

Variable	Variable Definition	Mean / Proportion	Standard deviation
TRANSF	Last year's transfers to home country (1000 Marks)	2.7	5.1
TRANSF_FAM	Transfers to support family at home	1.4	2.9
TRANSF_SAV	Transfers to build up savings at home (base category = for other reasons)	0.7	3.4
Income variables			
HHLINC	Monthly net labor income of household head (1000 Marks)	1.7	1.0
RHINC	Other monthly net household income (1000 Marks)	1.1	1.6
Labor Market Situation			
UNEMP	Household head unemployed at date of interview = 1	7.4	-.-
UNEMP_DUR	UNEMP interacted with cumulated unemployment duration within last year, DUR	0.5	2.2
SPUNEMP	Spouse unemployed = 1	3.3	-.-

individuals = 1330; # observations = 4668

While most of the variables are self-explanatory, given the above discussion on the determinants of return migration, some may warrant further comment.

- Since the number of female household heads is rather small in our sample, we did not split the sample by gender or experiment with interacting this variable with other variables in the model, but instead controlled for sex by simply including a gender dummy as an explanatory variable in the model.
- Age is interacted with a dummy variable with a value of one for individuals older than 50 years, and a value of zero otherwise, to take into account potential differences in behavior of older guest workers.
- The variable SECGEN takes on a value of one if the foreigner attended primary school in Germany, which implies that he or she was either born in Germany or migrated at a very early age.
- Aside from the total amount of last year's transfers to the home country, we also distinguish two other types of transfers, with *for other reasons* as the base category. TRANS_FAM is an indicator for *social integration*, TRANS_SAV for the savings motive mentioned above.
- The household head's net monthly labor income is interacted with dummy variables for nationality, in order to allow for different effects of earnings on an individual's expected duration of stay in Germany.

- Gross net household income is divided into the household head's net wage income and other income of the household, in order to allow for differences in behavior with respect to this variable. The latter variable also contains interest income on savings, and thus acts as a proxy for household wealth.
- The household head's cumulative unemployment is calculated by adding the durations of all unemployment spells within the twelve months before the date of interview in each wave, where spells may be both left and right censored. This variable is interacted with an individual's employment status at the date of interview. Thus, duration of unemployment in the past only has an effect on an individual's expected duration of stay if he or she is unemployed at the date of interview. This variable also enters with its square to allow for non-linear effects of unemployment duration.

For the following reasons we do not include potential earnings or indicators for macroeconomic conditions in guest workers' home countries as potential determinants for their expected duration variables in Germany. First, there is no information on a guest workers expected earnings in the home country, and even simple measures of average earnings or macroeconomic indicators such as unemployment, inflation, profitabiltiy etc. are not readily available for all source countries under consideration. Second, the importance a guest worker attaches to the latter indicators depends, to a large extent, on his or her economic and social status back home. Finally, even if these indicators were available, it is not obvious that they would give much more information than could be obtained by simply including dummies for time, nationality and some interaction terms, as we have done for the earnings variable (see below).

3 Econometric Specification

The purpose of the econometric model described in this section is to explain a guest worker's intention to stay in Germany. As argued in the previous section, we do not observe an exact indicator for this intention, but only know whether or not an individual's expected duration of stay falls within one of four broad categories measured on an ordinal scale, i.e. short-term, mid-term, long-term and permanent. Individual decisions can therefore be described by a discrete choice model with an ordered response variable. The econometric model takes into account both the nature of the dependent variable as an ordered categorical variable and individual effects, by exploiting the panel structure of our data base, which should contribute to more efficient parameter estimates.

We model an individual's intention to re-migrate in period t as a continuous latent variable, y_{it}^*, given by

(1) $\quad y_{it}^* = \beta' x_{it} + u_{it} \qquad i = 1, 2, \ldots N; \quad t = 1, 2, \ldots T_i$

where x_{it} is a vector of K explanatory variables (not including a constant), β a corresponding coefficient vector and u_{it} an error term which is composed of a time-constant individual effect, ε_i, and an error component, ω_{it}, which varies both between individuals and over time, i.e.

(2) $\quad u_{it} = \varepsilon_i + \omega_{it}$

with $\quad \varepsilon_i \sim N(0, \sigma_\varepsilon^2); \qquad \omega_{it} \sim N(0, \sigma_\omega^2)$

$E(\varepsilon_i, \omega_{jt}) = 0 \quad \forall i, j, t; \qquad E(\omega_{it}, \omega_{jt'}) = 0 \quad \forall i, j, t' \neq t$

$u_{it} \sim N(0, \sigma_u^2) \quad \text{with } \sigma_u^2 = \sigma_\varepsilon^2 + \sigma_w^2$

where N denotes the normal distribution function. The error components are assumed to be uncorrelated with x_{it}, $\forall i, t$.

Since in period t we only observe individuals who have not re-migrated, our sample is selected with respect to the actual re-migration decision, which gives rise to a potential self-selectivity bias. Given that there are very few re-migrants in each single year within the observation period, and that the potential selectivity bias resulting from the exclusion of return-migrants therefore seems of minor quantitative importance, we do not attempt to correct for it here[2]. Hence, we implicitly assume that sample attrition due to return migration (and for other reasons as well) occurs at random.

Let y_i be an indicator variable with values y_i = 1, 2, 3, 4 and define constants α_l, l = 0, 1, 2, 3, 4, with $\alpha_0 = -\infty$ and $\alpha_4 = +\infty$. For convenience, the time index is neglected for the moment. The probability, Pr, that an individual's intention to re-migrate falls into one of the four categories defined above is, after normalization, given by (see, e.g., Maddala, 1983: 47)

---

[2] Another reason that we do not attempt to correct for sample attrition here is that a standard two-step selectivity-correction procedure could potentially lead to inconsistent parameter estimates due to the non-linearity of the equation for the expected duration of stay discussed below.

(3) $\Pr(y_i = 1) = \Phi(\tilde{\alpha}_1 - \tilde{\beta}'x_i)$
$\Pr(y_i = 2) = \Phi(\tilde{\alpha}_2 - \tilde{\beta}'x_i) - \Phi(\tilde{\alpha}_1 - \tilde{\beta}'x_i)$
$\Pr(y_i = 3) = \Phi(\tilde{\alpha}_3 - \tilde{\beta}'x_i) - \Phi(\tilde{\alpha}_2 - \tilde{\beta}'x_i)$
$\Pr(y_i = 4) = 1 - \Phi(\tilde{\alpha}_3 - \tilde{\beta}'x_i)$

where Φ is the standard normal distribution function and $\tilde{\alpha}_l = \alpha / \sigma_u$, $\tilde{\beta} = \beta / \sigma_u$. Note that we have assumed equality of σ_u^2 in each period here.

Given that the assumptions on the error components in eq. (2) define an ordered probit model, the likelihood function for period t can be written as

(4) $L_t = \prod_{i=1}^{N} \prod_{l=1}^{4} \left(\Phi(\tilde{\alpha}_{l,t} - \tilde{\beta}'_t x_{i,t}) - \Phi(\tilde{\alpha}_{l-1,t} - \tilde{\beta}'_t x_{i,t}) \right)^{\delta_{ilt}}$

with $\delta_{ilt} = \begin{cases} 1 & \text{if } y_i \text{ falls into category } l \text{ in period } t \\ 0 & \text{otherwise} \end{cases}$

The likelihood function for the whole sample is then determined by simply multiplying the period-specific likelihood functions, i.e.

(5) $\bar{L} = \prod_{t=1}^{T_i} L_t$

where T_i is the number of periods individual i is observed in the sample. T_i varies among individuals due to sample attrition.

Given the distributional assumptions in (2), consistent estimates of the β coefficients can be obtained by maximizing either the likelihood function in eq. (4) for a single cross-section or the likelihood function in eq. (5) for the pooled sample. Following Chamberlain (1984), more efficient estimates can be obtained if the correlation between the error terms is taken into account by the following two-stage estimation procedure.

In the first step, consistent estimates for β_t based on eq. (4) are obtained for each single cross section. Then, an estimate for the asymptotic variance-covariance matrix of $\beta = (\beta_1, ..., \beta_T)$ is calculated which is given by

(6) $(\hat{\beta}) = \Lambda = (D' \Psi^{-1} D)^{-1}$

with $D_t = -\partial^2 \ln L_t / \partial \beta_t \partial \beta'_t$

where $D = diag\{D_1, ..., D_T\}$

and $\Psi = (\Psi_{s,t})_{s,t=1}^{T}$

with $\Psi_{s,t} = E\left[(\partial \ln L_s / \partial \beta_s)' (\partial \ln L_t / \partial \beta_t) \right]$.

$\Psi_{s,t}$ is estimated by the corresponding empirical sample moments; D_t can be calculated by exploiting the fact that the information matrix and the inverse of the variance-covariance matrix are asymptotically equivalent.

In the second step, this estimated variance-covariance matrix is then used as a weighing matrix in the minimum distance estimation, where the following function is minimized

$$(7) \quad \min_\theta \left[\hat{\beta} - g(\theta)\right]' \hat{\Lambda}^{-1} \left[\hat{\beta} - g(\theta)\right]$$

where θ is the $(K \times 1)$ coefficient vector in the panel probit and $g(\theta) = \iota \otimes \theta$, with ι a $(T \times 1)$ vector of ones. Note that the α_{it} do not enter eq. (7) and are thus allowed to vary between cross sections. In this way, we try to control for changes in the economic environment affecting all individuals between different time periods, in a way similar to including time dummies in a pooled regression model, which is not possible here due to the specification of the ordered probit model.

A consistent estimate of the variance-covariance matrix of θ is given by

$$(8) \quad V(\hat{\theta}) = (\hat{G}' \hat{\Lambda}^{-1} \hat{G})$$

with $\hat{G} = \partial g(\hat{\theta}) / \partial \theta'$.

Tests of hypotheses can be based on the distance function, DIS, in equation (9), evaluated at $\hat{\theta}$, which follows a χ^2 distribution with k degrees of freedom, where k is equal to the number of variables in the model. The test statistic is

$$(9) \quad DIS_{H_1} - DIS_{H_0} \sim \chi^2(k_{H_1} - k_{H_0})$$

where H_0 is the null and H_1 the alternative hypothesis.

4 Empirical Results

Following the two-stage estimation procedure outlined in the previous section, we first estimated reduced-form ordered-probit models for each year separately and then corrected the variance-covariance matrix based on these estimates in the second step. The estimated coefficient of a particular explanatory variable shows the relative effect of this variable on the intensity to re-migrate, i.e. on y_{it}^*. Estimation results for the random effects ordered Probit Model are given in Table 3. For the sake of comparison, estimation results for the simple pooling model are given in Table A1 in the appendix. Note that we have included time dummies for

1985 to 1989, with 1984 as the reference period, in the pooled model in order to allow for changes in the economic environment affecting all individuals similarly.

For most variables, the two estimation procedures yield qualitatively similar results. Since the random effects panel probit model gives more efficient parameter estimates than the simple pooling model, without requiring very severe additional assumptions, we prefer the former specification and restrict the following discussion to the estimation results summarized in Table 3.

To start with the personal characteristics, the effect of gender on an individual's expected duration of stay is statistically insignificant. This may be due to the relatively small number of female household heads in our sample. As shown by the χ^2-tests in the last column of the table, both age variables and their squares are statistically significant. For both age groups, the age effect is negative within the relevant range, where the negative effect is much stronger for the older age group. Thus, the implied age pattern is consistent with the hypothesis that the probability of return migration increases as guest workers approach the retirement age.

Relative to guest workers for Turkey, who make up the reference category, national differences are only significant for those from former Yugoslavia, who intend to stay longer in Germany. Higher education also increases an individual's expected duration of stay significantly, which can be explained by the more restricted transferability of specific human capital to the home country. While being married with a spouse living in Germany has no statistically significant effect on this variable, the presence of children in the age groups of 6 to 15 years increases the household head's expected duration of stay significantly.

The latter result can be explained by the desire of guest workers with young children to have them complete school in Germany. On the other hand, having grown-up children (older than 18 years) in Germany increases the expected duration of stay of the household head. Given that most second-generation foreigners in this age group do not intend to return to their parent's home country, this result is compatible with the hypothesis that older household heads chose their residence within a household context, which implies that the number of permanent stayers among guest workers will increase with the proportion of second-generation foreigners in Germany[3]. Whether or not a guest worker has severe health problems and has officially been testified as disabled does not affect his re-migration decision. Because provision of health care in Germany is relatively well developed, this is a somewhat unexpected result given that we control for potential intervening factors, unemployment in particular.

---

[3] The importance of the link between the first and second generation of guest workers in Germany for the duration of stay of the former is also stressed by Backhaus-Maul/Vogel (1992), referring to recent research on the social integration of older guest workers in Germany.

Table 3: Determinants of Expected Duration of Stay; Panel Random Effects ordered Probit Model, 1984 - 1989

Variable	Coefficient	|t|	χ^2 (d.o.f.)
Personal Characteristics			
SEX	0.1214	1.32	
AGE	0.0020	0.03	
AGESQ/100	-0.0153	0.17	23.97*(2)
AGE50	0.0348	0.83	
AGE50SQ/100	-0.0808	2.24*	49.02*(2)
NATY	0.2169	1.97*	
NATG	-0.0652	0.45	
NATI	0.1171	0.97	
NATS	0.0307	0.19	
EDUC_LOW	0.0739	1.30	
EDUC_HIGH	0.1462	1.96*	
MARRIED	-0.0552	0.79	
CHILD_5	-0.0141	0.26	
CHILD_15	0.1505	2.83*	
CHILD_16	-0.0388	0.74	
CHILD_19	0.1140	2.00*	
DISABLED	0.0335	0.38	
Integration indicators			
YSM	0.0179	0.95	
YSMSQ/100	0.0259	0.47	40.31*(2)
SECGEN	-0.2392	1.08	
SPOUSE_A	-0.0751	0.75	
CHILD_A	-0.2561	3.82*	
SPEAK_B	0.1220	0.61	
SPEAK_G	-0.0762	1.01	
GSPEAK_B	-0.2111	3.99*	
GSPEAK_G	0.1819	4.04*	
FEEL_B	-0.1996	2.82*	
FEEL_G	0.1814	4.36*	
OWNER	0.3510	3.12*	
Transfers			
TRANSF	-0.0245	4.00*	
TRANSF_FAM	-0.0073	0.90	
TRANSF_SAV	0.0027	0.33	

Table 3 continued

Variable	Coefficient	|t|	χ^2 (d.o.f.)
	Income variables		
HHLINC	-0.0343	0.78	
HHLINC_Y	0.0311	0.58	
HHLINC_G	-0.0128	0.17	29,40*(4)
HHLINC_I	0.0116	0.20	
HHLINC_S	0.0613	0.78	
RHINC	-0.0235	1.73*	
	Labor Market Situation		
UNEMP	-0.2724	1.98*	14,56*(2)
UNEMP_DUR	0.0595	1.25	
UNEMP_DURSQ	-0.0034	0.95	
SPUNEMP	-0.2364	2.65*	

Distance-statistic: $\chi^2(42) = 300.23$; # observations = 4668
Note: Test statistics are marked by an asterisk if significant at the 5% level

Turning to the assimilation indicators, we find that the expected duration of stay in Germany increases, at an increasing rate, with the number of years since migration. This result strongly supports the hypothesis that guest workers become more integrated into German sociey the longer they have been in Germany. Somewhat surprisingly, belonging to the "second generation", i.e. either having been born or having attended primary school in Germany, seems to have no significant effect on an individual's expected duration of stay, which is probably due to the small number of individuals falling into this category.

While having a spouse in the home country does not, per se, significantly affect a guest worker's re-migration decision, having children abroad has a strong negative effect on his or her expected duration of stay in Germany, as would be expected. Because these two variables are strongly correlated, their effects should be interpreted together as joint influences on having a family in the home country. The result that knowledge of the mother tongue does not significantly affect an individual's decision to re-migrate is probably due to the small number of foreigners in our sample with only a poor knowlege of their mother tongue. In contrast, knowledge of the German language, which seems to be a strong indicator for integration in society, has a relatively strong effect. Similarily, a guest worker's subjective feeling about Germany has a strong effect on his intention to stay or return. Finally, owning a house or apartment in Germany has a very strong positive effect on a foreigner's expected duration of stay. This also is compatible with the hypothesis that the more integrated a guest worker is in German society the longer his or her expected duration of stay.

As expected, the higher a guest worker's transfers to the home country the shorter his or her expected duration of stay in Germany. This result complements the one reported in a study by Dustmann (1992) who showed that a dummy variable for transfers has a positive effect on a guest worker's expected duration of stay in Germany but did not consider how this effect varies with the amount transferred. In order to test whether the effect differs between transfers to support the family and transfers to build up savings at home, we have distinguished between these two possibilities but found no statistically significant difference between them.

Given our specification of the interaction terms of the household head's wage income with dummies for nationality, estimation results show that the effect of wage income is not statistically significant for turkish people, while the interaction terms for the other groups are jointly significant. Adding the coefficient on HHINC to the respective coefficient on the interaction terms, which gives the overall effect of this variable on an individual's expected duration of stay, shows that for Italians and Greeks the effect is not much different from that for the turkish people and is virtually zero for guest workers from Yugoslavia and positive for Spaniards. These differences may arise due to different situations in home countries, i.e. differences in earnings differentials, and/or nation-specific responses to earnings differentials. As we do not observe potential earnings in the home countries, these effects cannot be identified. It should also be noted that the effects of both HHINC and the interaction terms cannot be estimated very accurately, as these variables are strongly correlated with YSM and the dummies for nationality. Other net household income, RHINC, significantly reduces an individual's expected duration of stay. Given that this variable includes interest income on wealth and thus acts as a proxy for savings, this result is compatible with the hypothesis that the re-migration decision is influenced by the savings motive.

Being unemployed at the date of interview lowers an individual's expected duration of stay significantly, a result which has also been obtained by Dustmann (1992), who interprets it as contradictory to the assertion that unemployed guest workers will not re-migrate as long as they can draw unemployment benefits. Given this interpretation, it seems natural not only to include the employment status at the date of interview, but also an individual's cumulated duration of unemployment within a reference period as explanatory variables in the model if he or she is unemployed at the date of interview. In order to allow for non-linear effects of this variable, its square is also included in the regression. Both interaction variables are jointly significant and imply that for durations up to approximately nine months, the effect on the expected duration of stay is positive and thereafter becomes negative. Although this result qualifies the above finding somewhat, in its interpretation one has to take into account that an individual's employment status and the duration variable are highly correlated. Finally, there is strong evidence for the hypothesis that spouses's unemployment also affects the decision of the household head to re-migrate.

5 Summary and Conclusion

We have analyzed guest workers' expected duration of stay in Germany within an econometric model taking into account the important distinction between permanent and temporary stayers, where the expected duration of stay for the latter has been differentiated in short-term, mid-term and long-term. The model has been estimated for household heads on the first six waves of the German Socio-Economic Panel, taking advantage of the panel structure of our data base to obtain efficient parameter estimates.

The estimation results show that, aside from certain personal characteristics – in particular age, nationality and education – the family structure has an important influence on the household head's expected duration of stay in Germany. Both the presence of children who have not yet completed school and the prescence of grown-up children significantly increase the household head's expected duration of stay. Other indicators for the degree of a guest worker's integration in German society, such as years since migration, the ability to speak German, the subjective feeling of well-being associated with the stay in Germany, whether or not the household head has a child in the home country, and whether or not he or she owns property in Germany, also significantly affect individual re-migration decisions. On the other hand, we find that the higher the amount of money a guest workers transfers to his or her home country, the shorter his/her expected duration of stay. We also find that the effect of the household head's wage income differs between source countries, and that the higher other household income, the shorter the expected duration of stay. Finally, an important result is that a guest worker's labor market position, in particular the incidence and duration of unemployment, has significant effects on an individual's expected duration of stay in Germany.

Given that individual expectations are, on the average, correct and/or determine actual re-migration behavior, these results should contribute to an understanding of the determinants of observed future outflows of migrants, which seems important for the implementation of an effective migration policy.

Appendix

Table A1: Determinants of Expected Duration of Stay; Pooled Ordered Probit Model, 1984 - 1989

Variable	Coefficient	|t|	χ² (d.o.f.)
	Personal Characteristics		
SEX	0.1030	1.53	
AGE	-0.0441	1.68	} 11.58*(2)
AGESQ	0.0436	1.26	
AGE50	-0.0049	0.30	} 39.60*(2)
AGE50SQ	-0.0391	2.58*	
NATY	0.3030	5.65*	
NATG	-0.2059	3.32*	
NATI	0.0572	1.09*	
NATS	0.0584	0.91	
EDUC_LOW	0.0705	1.88	
EDUC_HIGH	0.0540	1.07	
MARRIED	-0.0510	0.93	
CHILD_5	-0.0682	1.58	
CHILD_15	0.1323	3.44*	
CHILD_16	0.0349	0.74	
CHILD_19	0.1165	2.43*	
DISABLED	0.1183	1.65	
	Integration indicators		
YSM	-0.0041	0.32	} 47.10* (2)
YSMSQ	0.0897	2.48*	
SECGEN	0.0044	0.03	
SPOUSE_A	-0.1006	1.28	
CHILD_A	-0.2980	5.46	
SPEAK_B	-0.3060	0.17	
SPEAK_G	-0.1219	1.60	
GSPEAK_B	-0.2502	5.26	
GSPEAK_G	0.1848	4.80*	
FEEL_B	-0.1693	2.36*	
FEEL_G	0.2364	6.16*	
OWNER	0.5165	6.72*	
TRANSF	-0.0312	5.33*	
TRANSF_FAM	-0.0031	0.38	
TRANSF_SAV	0.0057	0.83	

Table A1 continued

Variable	Coefficient	|t|	χ^2 (d.o.f.)
	Income variable		
HHLINC	0.0744	0.54	
HHLINC_Y	0.1114	0.97	
HHLINC_G	-0.0227	0.36	11.82* (4)
HHLINC_I	-0.2261	2.17*	
HHLINC_S	0.3543	2.27*	
RHINC	-0.0289	2.44*	
	Labor Market Situation		
UNEMP	-0.2515	1.79	
UNEMP_DUR	0.0070	0.14	4.4 (2)
UNEMP_DURSQ	0.0016	0.42	
SPUNEMP	-0.1874	2.15*	
	Year Dummies		
DUM 85	0.0175	0.35	
DUM 86	-0.0015	0.03	
DUM 87	0.0415	0.78	
DUM 88	0.1507	2.64*	
DUM 89	0.2279	3.60*	

Likelihood-ratio statistic: $\chi^2(47) = 907,94$; # observations = 4668
Note: Test statistics are marked by an asterisk if significant at the 5% level

References

Backhaus-Maul, H./D. Vogel (1992): Vom ausländischen Arbeitnehmer zum Rentner - Ausgewählte Aspekte der finanziellen Absicherung und sozialen Versorgung alter Ausländer in der Bundesrepublik Deutschland; Zeitschrift für Gerontologie, 25, 166-177.

Brecht, Beatrix (1990): Türkische Remigranten: Untersuchungen am Datensatz des Sozio-ökonomischen Panels; Diskussionsbeiträge Serie II - Nr. 125, Sonderforschungsbereich 178, Universität Konstanz.

Chamberlain, Gary (1984): Panel Data; in: Z. Griliches/M.D. Intriligator, Handbook of Econometrics, Vol. II, Chapter 22; North Holland.

Djajic, Slobodan/Ross Milbourne (1988): A general equlibrium model of guest workers migration. The source country perspective; Journal of International Economics 25, 335-351.

Dustmann, Christian (1992): Do we stay or not? Return decisions of temporary migrants; Mimeo, European University Institute, San Domenica di Fiesole.

Hönekopp, Elmar (1987): Rückkehrförderung und Rückkehr ausländischer Arbeitnehmer - Ergebnisse des Rückkehrförderungsgesetzes, der Rückkehrhilfe-Statistik und der IAB-Rückkehrerbefragung; in: E. Hönekopp (Ed.), Aspekte der Ausländerbeschäftigung in der Bundesrepublik Deutschland, BeitrAB 114, Nürnberg.

Licht, Georg/Viktor Steiner (1992): Assimiliation, labor market experience, and earnings profiles of temporary and permanent immigrant workers in Germany; Discussion Paper No. 93-06, ZEW, Mannheim.

Maddala, G. (1982): Limited-dependent and Qualitative Variables in Econometrics; Cambridge University Press, Cambridge.

Münzenmaier, Werner/Ilse Walter (1983): Ausländische Haushalte in Baden-Württemberg - Rückkehrabsichten, Familiennachzug und Integration; Zeitschrift für Bevölkerungswissenschaft, 9, 487-496.

Rendtel, Ulrich (1992): On the Choice of a Selection-Model When Estimating Regression Models With Selectivity; Discussion Paper No. 53, DIW Berlin.

Wagner, Gert/Jürgen Schupp/Ulrich Rendtel (1991): The Socio-Economic Panel (SOEP) for Germany - Methods of Production and Management of Longitudinal Data; Discussion Paper No. 31a, DIW Berlin.

Werth, Manfred (1983): Rückkehr- und Verbleibabsichten türkischer Arbeitnehmer; MittAB 4/1983, 345 - 359.

Unemployment and Attitudes Towards Foreigners in Germany[1]

Ira N. Gang
Economics Department - NJH, Rutgers University
New Brunswick, NJ 08903-5055, USA

Francisco L. Rivera-Batiz
Department of Economics and Teachers College,
Columbia University
New York, NY 10027, USA

1 Introduction

Germany has a long history of attracting immigrants. This is reflected in the substantial portion of the population accounted for by immigrants. In 1989, foreigners constituted between 7.3% and 7.9% of the population in West Germany.[2] This figure, however, underestimates the inflows of population: In the German statistics, foreigners do not include foreign-born who are ethnic German or foreign-born who have received a German passport. In addition to the inflow of "foreigners," there has been a large migration of ethnic Germans to West Germany since World War II (before 1950 the inflow was more than 12 million; between 1950 and 1988 it was 4.8 million; and between 1989 and 1990, 0.779 million). Therefore, the number of foreign-born persons in Germany is comparatively high.[3] This was conscious policy choice. Germany has a "law of return" for "ethnic" Germans and a long history of actively attracting "guestworkers."[4]

---

[1] Parts of the paper were presented in a seminar at the Directorate for Economic and Financial Affairs of the European Commission in Brussels on March 1, 1993. The authors are grateful to the comments of the participants of the workshop. The authors also wish to acknowledge the valuable computer assistance of Edwin Milan. We also thank both editors of this volume for their detailed and useful comments.
[2] Different sources provide different estimates.
[3] In the United States, for instance, the proportion of the foreign-born in the population hovered around 6.2% in 1980 and was 7.9% in 1990. In Europe, only Luxembourg and Switzerland have substantially higher proportions; see Simon (1986), pp. 20-21.
[4] Although the German "guestworker" policy characterized migrants as "temporary," by 1987 close to 40 percent of the "foreign-born" in Germany had

The recent wave of anti-foreigner violence has been viewed as a reaction to this population movement. Germany's unification has had severe economic repercussions, perhaps none so harsh as those in the labor market. The closing of firms in the new federal states displaced workers from their jobs, giving rise to a large increase in open unemployment (see Layard et. al., 1992). In East Germany, official unemployment raged at 14.7% of the labor force in early 1993, with unofficial estimates much higher than that. Unification also brought with it the opportunity for workers to move west - since 1989 over one million people have migrated from the new federal states. In 1991 alone over 200,000 people from the east migrated to the west. New international immigration from the rest of Eastern Europe and other areas added to the potential displacement of both western and eastern workers in Germany. Newspaper reports tell of many activities and acts of violence directed against the foreign-born, and there are some indications of resentment in the west toward easterners.[5]

The popular presumption is that immigrants are substituting for native-born laborers. That is, immigrants are depressing wages and displacing native-born workers - i.e., they are causing native-born unemployment. This presumption has very strong policy implications and is implicit in the recent calls for increased regulation of immigration. Yet, there is mixed evidence on the impact of immigration on those already present in the German labor market. For instance, economists John P. DeNew and Klaus F. Zimmermann, having studied the West German Socioeconomic Panel data, conclude that immigrants are substitutes for blue collar and complements for white collar workers.[6] Our own joint work using Eurobarometer survey data suggests that the impact of most immigrant groups into Germany is likely to have minor impact on the income earned by most German residents.[7] On the other hand, research on the impact of immigrants on unemployment has yielded some negative effects of immigration on the employment of German residents (see Winkelmann and Zimmermann, 1993 and Franz, Oser and Winker, 1993).

Immigrants, and more generally, foreigners, are the first to feel the wrath of other workers during times of economic stress. Conventional wisdom tells us that those most hurt by immigration are more likely to hate foreigners and hence have the strongest reaction against them. Time and time again in both the popular press and in academic discourse we hear reports that the acts of ethnic violence or bias that foreigners experience in the host countries arise largely because

---

been there over 15 years. This is in spite of policies during the 1980's to encourage the emigration of guestworkers, such as the Rueckkehrhilfegesetz of 1983.

[5] The Economist, Feb 15, 1992 reported a tenfold increase between 1990 and 1991 in recorded attacks on foreigners to almost 200 a month. On February 15, 1993, a New York Times article reported that, during 1992, more than 2,000 attacks against foreigners were recorded.

[6] DeNew and Zimmermann (1993), p. 1.

[7] See Gang and Rivera-Batiz (1993).

their presence irritates the economically disaffected. The economically disaffected are thus held to be at the root of hate crimes against immigrants. If this is so, then the logical implication is that the unemployed should have the most negative reaction to foreigners amongst the population. If they do not, on the other hand, one would have to conclude that either immigration is not critically affecting the unemployment of the native-born or, otherwise, that non-economic variables - such as prejudice and discrimination - are the stronger motivators of negative attitudes toward foreigners.

In this paper we examine the effect of foreign presence on the employment status of native-born German citizens. We also examine attitudes toward foreigners displayed by individuals in various labor market situations. This allows us to explore the determinants of attitudes toward foreigners - that is, whether negative attitudes toward immigrants are related to the labor market or economic situation, or whether they are independent of labor market status and thus related to non-economic variables, such as prejudice and ethnic bias[8]. Although we concentrate on Germany in this paper, we emphasize that anti-immigrant feelings have been expressed in other EEC countries (as well as in many other nations all over the world). Indeed, our analysis of opinion survey responses below will show that, compared to some countries with lower amounts of immigration, Germany has a smaller proportion of the population whose perception is that there are too many foreigners, or that foreigners increase their unemployment.

In the next section we offer some background on German immigration and describe the nature of the Eurobarometer survey data set we use. Section III presents our analysis of the determinants of unemployment and of the impact of foreign presence on the employment of German residents. In Section IV we provide an overview of European attitudes toward foreigners, and examine how these attitudes vary among several European countries. For Germany, in Section V we look at how attitudes vary by employment status, and provide a preliminary analysis of the factors 'determining' the attitudes of German residents toward foreigners. Section VI summarizes our results.

---

[8] Our approach is to use unemployment as a proxy for both the economic status of the individual and general economic conditions. Of course, other specific economic reasons--such as a housing shortage--might play a role in attitude formation.

2 Background on German Immigration and the Euro-Barometer Data Set

Table 1 provides the distribution of foreigners in western Germany in 1989. In that year, 7.7% of the population in western Germany was classified as foreigner. The single largest immigrant group has its ancestry in Turkey, from where 1,612,623 workers had located in western Germany by 1989. The second largest immigrant group came from Yugoslavia, from where 610,499 persons were residing in western Germany during 1989. A large portion of these foreigners formed part of immigrant waves to Germany in the 1960s and 1970s: fully 1/4 of the 4,845,882 foreigners in Germany in 1989 had been living there for more than 20 years, and 1/2 for at least 15 years (TWIG, July 17, 1992).

The late 1980s saw the reemergence of mass migration to Germany. Between 1988 and the end of 1991, western Germany experienced the largest influx of foreigners since the early 1950s. Of 3.2 million net immigrants in this period, 1.4 were foreigners, and 1.8 were ethnic German "resettlers".[9] Most of the newcomers went to southern German states - particularly Baden Wuerttemberg, where 5.9 percent of the population is made up of persons who arrived between 1988 and 1991. In Hamburg the percentage is 5.7%, while in the Saarland it is 2.7% (TWIG, December 18, 1992).

In the press, in some policy circles and in public discussions this sudden immigration was held responsible for economic hard times. While this may be true, there does not appear to be a simple correlation between the presence of the foreign-born workers and unemployment. Indeed, although we have just seen that western Germany saw a dramatic rise in immigrant flows during the late 1980s and early 1990s, the unemployment rate in the western part of Germany during this period fell, from 8.9% in 1985 to 7.6% in 1989 and to 6.6% in December 1992.

Does the presence of foreigners affect the labor market status of native-born Germans? Do the employed, unemployed, students, retirees, and those out of the labor force differ in their attitudes toward foreigners? These are highly complex questions that require economic - and non-economic - analysis in many fronts. We attempt here to make some headway, however incomplete, by studying, first, whether higher concentrations of foreign-born workers are correlated with higher unemployment among native-born residents, and, second, whether negative attitudes toward foreigners among Germans are related to employment status.

---

[9] These numbers do not include asylum seekers. The number of asylum applications to Western European governments increased sharply in the 1980s and early 1990s, from a total of 67,400 in 1983 to nearly 700,000 in 1992.

Table 1: Foreigners in West Germany, 1989

Nationals of	
EUR-12 Member Countries	*1,325,400*
Belgium	18,697
Denmark	13,492
Greece	293,649
Spain	129,963
France	77,602
Ireland	8,872
Italy	519,548
Luxembourg	4,764
Netherlands	101,238
Portugal	74,890
United Kingdom	85,748
Other European Countries	*2,777,707*
Yugoslavia	610,499
Turkey	1,612,623
African Countries	*163,579*
Algeria	5,924
Morocco	61,848
Tunisia	24,292
Other Countries	*579,195*
USA	85,707
Canada	8,021
India	23,896
Japan	20,094
Total Non-Member Countries	3,520,482
Total Foreigners	*4,845,882*
Total Population	61,238,000

Source: Eurostat (1991): Demographic Statistics 1991. Luxembourg 1991.

What allows us to approach these questions is our use of the October/ November 1988 Eurobarometer Survey, which focused on finding out the attitudes of Europeans toward immigrant populations. The Eurobarometer surveys offer unique data sets consisting of a single cross section of a geographically distributed random sample of households across the twelve European Community countries (see Reif and Melich, 1991).[10] Launched in 1974, the surveys are con-

---

[10] Interviewing and sampling were conducted in Germany by the Institut fuer Markt und Meinungsforschung (EMNID), Bielefeld. A two-stage sampling

ducted in the Spring and Fall of each year to monitor the social and political attitudes of the public in the twelve European Community nations. We use the West German subsample of the October/November 1988 Eurobarometer survey. Besides information on household economic and demographic behavior, this Eurobarometer survey contains detailed questions on attitudes toward immigrants and foreigners. The data also contains information on whether the survey respondent was a citizen or not, also information on whether any immediate family member is Turkish, of other foreign origin, or not of foreign-origin.

For this study, we analyze the subgroup of citizens 16 years of age or older, not of foreign origin and not in the military. This is as close as the data allows us to distinguish a civilian, native-born German group. It is our belief that this is an important group to study, as most of the public discussion regarding the impact of immigrants refers to the opinions and attitudes of this group. We remove from the sample respondents who did not answer as to their nationality, occupation, age or sex, or who reported being in households where the number of adults was less than one. These deletions reduced our sample from 1051 respondents to 858 observations. While great care was taken by the Eurobarometer researchers to ensure a representative sample, the analysis presented in this paper is of course limited by how truly representative the sample is. Opinion surveys, due to their great expense in time and effort, tend to rely on a relatively small number of observations - when compared to census-type surveys. Because of this shortcoming, after outlining the issues using cross-tabulations (Tables 4, 5, 6, and 7), we then apply rigorous econometric tests to establish the statistical significance of our results (Table 8).

Table 2 presents a summary of the sample means of the major variables defined in our study. The average age in the sample of 858 respondents was equal to 43.59 years, education was equal to 11.19 years, and potential labor market experience (defined as the age of the person minus the age at which education was completed) was 26.58 years. The sample consists of 48% male respondents and 66% heads of households, with an average of 0.36 children in each household. A total of 7% of the sample thought that there were many foreigners living in their neighborhood, with 52% saying that there were only a few, and 41% saying none (on average, 7.7% of the population in the Eurobarometer sample consisted of non-citizens, which coincides with the estimates of the number of foreigners in west Germany quoted in the introduction).

---

method was used. In the first stage, a random selection of sampling points was made from the whole territory of west Germany. Various types of areas (urban, rural, etc.) were represented in proportion to their populations. Approximately 1,350 sampling points were selected. In the second stage, individual respondents were selected from the sampling points obtained in the first stage, by a "random route" methodology (a combination of selecting individuals at random from population registers and quota sampling in which census data was used to establish quotas by age, sex and occupation.

Table 2: Sample Means

Variables	Total Sample	Employed	Unemployed	Student	Out of Labor Force	Retired
Number of Cases	858	452	41	69	129	167
Age	43.6	38.0	36.1	21.9	47.4	66.5
Education (years)	11.2	11.2	10.5	n.a.	9.7	10.0
Potential Experience	26.6	20.8	19.6	0.0	31.7	50.4
Male	.48	.59	.44	.67	.03	.46
# Children Less Than 15	.36	.45	.22	.07	.69	.02
Head of Household	.66	.71	.78	.39	.26	.90
Presence of Foreigners	.077	.080	.076	.077	.073	.077
Employed	.53	1.0				
Unemployed	.05		1.0			
Student	.08			1.0		
Out of the Labor Force	.15				1.0	
Retired	.19					1.0
Many Foreigners in Neighborhood	.07	.06	.15	.07	.05	.08
A Few Foreigners in Neighborhood	.52	.55	.56	.64	.46	.44
No Foreigners in Neighborhood	.41	.39	.29	.29	.50	.47

Note: Data for variable "Presence of Foreigners" (% in region) from (SIBA, 1991). Numbers may not add to 100% due to rounding.

Source: Our calculations from the data (Reif and Melich, 1991).

An examination of the data presented in Table 2, which is disaggregated by labor market status, shows what initially grabbed our attention and led to the econometric analysis in this study. Some differences among the population groups in Table 2 are as expected. Students are younger than other groups and retirees are older, with a very high level of potential labor market experience (measured as age minus age at which education was completed). Students are not usually heads of household, while the retirees who answered the survey usually are. Those out of the labor force are predominantly female living in households with children less than 15 years old. The unemployed - as well as those out of the labor force - have lower educational levels than the employed. There are, in addition, some not-so-obvious patterns in the data. For instance, the employed have more children then the unemployed, perhaps suggesting economic necessity drives them to have greater attachment to jobs. Also, heads of household have a higher likelihood of being unemployed relative to being employed. This may be due a sampling problem: due to their greater availability, unemployed heads of household are usually more likely to respond to the survey than employed heads of household.

We are particularly interested in the responses of the persons sampled to a question asking individuals to self-report their impression of the number of foreigners in their neighborhood. A total of 6% of the employed, 7% of students, 5% of out of the labor force, 8% of retirees, but 15% of the unemployed reported "many foreigners." Given that the actual foreign population was equal to 7.7%, one is puzzled about what explains the much greater presence of foreigners (almost twice) reported by unemployed persons in their neighborhood. Is this because the unemployed happen to live in neighborhoods where foreigners also live? Or is it that the unemployed perceive that there are more foreigners around, but this is not really the case?

The Eurobarometer data that we are utilizing was gathered from October through November 1988 in West Germany. While this limits the applicability of our results to the current unified Germany, we believe it still allows us to offer some important insights. In some sense, the sampling period can be considered more stable - economically and socially - than the period afterwards, in which the upheavals of unification could have acted to disturb public opinion in unpredictable ways. Moreover, if attitudes in this sample period are found anti-foreigner, we would expect a recent intensification of these feelings, given the massive migratory flows during the last three years.

Before discussing attitudes, we first explore the question of whether the presence of foreigners can be linked to unemployment among German citizens.

3 The Employment of German Residents and the Presence of Foreign Workers

The employment effects of foreigners are highly relevant to an understanding of German attitudes toward the foreign-born. If unemployment among German citizens becomes greater because of the presence of foreign workers, then it is easy to understand the existence of resentment - and negative attitudes - of unemployed workers toward foreigners. Although we cannot really explore the issue of causality between unemployment and foreign presence using cross-sectional data, we can examine the partial correlation between the two variables. In this Section we report the results of our analysis of whether foreign presence affects employment status.

There is substantial evidence showing that immigrant participation in host country labor markets is quite complex and in many ways different from that of native-born citizens. Studies of immigrants in the United States show that the foreign-born tend to earn wages substantially below those of comparable native-born workers when they initially enter the economy (see Chiswick, 1978); Borjas, 1990). Partly, this is the result of adjustment costs, such as inadequate language skills or knowledge of the host country labor market (see Rivera-Batiz, 1990; Chiswick, 1993; Dustmann, 1993; Licht and Steiner, 1992; Pischke, 1992 and Beenstock, 1993). As length of time in the host country increases, though, assimilation occurs and immigrant earnings tend to approach those of comparable native-born workers (see Borjas, 1985 and Lalonde and Topel, 1992). Indeed, the labor market behavior of recent immigrants in Germany does appear to differ, at least initially, from that of workers already in the market. For instance, Ulrich (1991) finds that the labor force participation rate is higher for new immigrants. This pattern is related to the age and sex structure of the new immigrant population (young, male workers), and it changes as migrant stay in the host country lengthens. As immigrants suffer the initial disadvantages in earnings caused by entry into a new labor market (see Schmidt, 1992a,b), their labor force participation becomes comparatively high, but as they assimilate into the host country economy, their labor force participation tends to converge to that of the native-born. This is observed in the changes among the German female immigrant labor force. From 1974 to 1988 the foreign-born female labor force participation rate in Germany fell from 46 percent to 37 percent. For native-born Germans it rose in this period from 30 percent to 37 percent.

Occupational structure differs widely between the foreign-born and native-born. About one-fourth of the foreign-born laborers work in unskilled occupations. For the native-born, less than 5 percent are employed as unskilled laborers. By contrast, less than 3 percent of foreign-born laborers can be found in white collar jobs, compared to over 20 percent of the native-born. A more detailed breakdown finds that 35 percent of Turkish-born workers in Germany are in semi-skilled jobs. Among the Yugoslav-born immigrants, only 19 percent are in unskilled jobs, while 26 percent are in skilled jobs. It seems that older immigrant groups more closely reflect the job distribution of native-born Germans (see Krueger and Pischke, 1992 for a comparison of west and East German workers).

Considering the complex labor market status of the foreign-born in any host country, one must warn against hastily assuming that immigrants automatically increase unemployment of the native-born. The economic theory of the impact of immigration does not predict that immigration is necessarily linked to greater unemployment among the native-born. It is true that in a simple rigid wage model where the labor market is homogeneous, increased immigration will raise labor supply and thus increase unemployment. However, in more complex models, the impact of immigration on unemployment in any given labor market is ambiguous. For instance, in some versions of the Harris-Todaro model,[11] immigration into a competitive labor market tends to reduce wages in that market and induce native-born workers to emigrate into higher-paying, rigid-wage labor markets, thus raising unemployment in the latter. Since immigrant concentration in a particular labor market may lead the unemployed native-born workers to relocate to other labor markets one would not see a direct linkage between local unemployment and immigration, rather, immigration into one region may lead to unemployment in other regions (see Rivera-Batiz, 1981). Empirically, therefore, one would not observe areas of foreign concentration being linked to greater native-born unemployment. Unfortunately, this type of effect is hard to detect econometrically (for a recent attempt, see Filer, 1992).

Immigrants could raise the employment of the native-born if they are complementary with native-born workers. By the definition of input complementarity, if native-born workers are complements to immigrants, the foreign labor inflow increases the demand for native-born labor, thus raising rather than lowering the employment of native workers.[12] In Germany, this may be the case if unskilled immigrants are complements to skilled German workers.

We now discuss our empirical analysis of the effects of the presence of foreigners on the labor market status of native-born citizens. Our approach is to estimate a reduced form probit equation for the probability of employment - versus unemployment - among native-born workers in Germany using Eurobarometer household level (respondent) data. We thus estimate how various determinants of employment affect the likelihood that a German resident will be

---

[11] See Gang and Gangopadhyay (1987) and (1985) and Dutta, Gang and Gangopadhyay (1989) for an analysis of the Harris-Todaro model and the impact of government policies on employment; see also Gang and Tower (1990) for a discussion of the modeling of employment in a search model.

[12] For a discussion of the issue of complementarity between immigrant and native-born workers, see Gang and Rivera-Batiz (1993), Rivera-Batiz and Sechzer (1991), Borjas (1983,1986), Grossman (1982), Bean, Lowell and Taylor (1988), Card (1990), LaLonde and Topel (1991), and Matta and Popp (1985).

employed relative to being unemployed (see Beggs and Chapman, 1990 and Rivera-Batiz, 1992 for applications of this approach). Among these variables, we include foreign presence in the local labor market where the German worker is located. We will thus determine whether there is an effect of foreign presence in the labor market on the probability of employment of native-born citizens, after controlling for differences in skill (schooling and potential labor market experience) and for demographic characteristics (gender, presence of children, head of household).

Our dependent variable is a qualitative variable, equal to one if the person is employed and zero if unemployed. Our sample is thus restricted to those in the labor force, i.e., the employed and the unemployed. Unemployment in the sample encompasses approximately 10% of the labor force, which is somewhat above the official estimates for 1988, which hovered around 8%. This oversampling is often found in non-economic household surveys in which some individuals out of the labor force end-up catalogued as unemployed. Given the great extent of switching between individuals in and out of the labor force, the bias introduced by the over-sampling of the unemployed in the survey is very unlikely to significantly bias our results.

The likelihood of employment tends to be greater among those who have a larger stock of skills relevant to the labor market. One element is education, quantified by years of schooling (measured in the survey by the age at which the person left school minus 6). On-the-job experience is a second form of human capital: Experience represents the acquisition of skills on-the-job or through learning by doing, leading to higher marginal productivity. Years of labor market experience or on the job training are also associated with lower quit and layoff rates. We measure the maximum potential labor market experience of an individual as his/her age minus the age at which the person left school.

The extent of employment varies systematically by certain demographic characteristics, and we must control statistically for these effects. Employment rates tend to be greater among men - holding other things equal - partly because labor force attachment among men is higher, which lowers their reservation wages and raises the likelihood that they will take a given job opportunity. This also applies to heads of household. In addition, respondents coming from households with more children are expected to have a greater attachment to employment: they simply cannot afford sustained spells of unemployment and, with a lower reservation wage, they are more likely to accept job offers, everything else constant.

We use two measures to capture foreign presence. The first is the actual percentage of population in the region (Bundesländer) where the person is located that is foreign (SIBA, 1991).[13] This variable we call FORPRES in our analysis

---

[13] The Eurobarometer data only allows us to identify each household by state (Bundesländer), not county (Kreis). The extent to which the variation in foreign presence within a state affects labor market status of the household is not addressed by this variable.

below. The second measure of foreign presence is based on the respondents self-report of foreign presence, elicited in response to the question "are there many, a few or no people of another nationality who live in your neighborhood?". In our estimation below, we include two variables: MANY, if the person responded that there were many foreigners in their neighborhood, and FEW, if the person said that there were few foreigners in their neighborhood. This measure of foreign presence obviously contains a large amount of measurement error as it relies on respondents' perceptions, but that is exactly why it may be more interesting.

To summarize our empirical model, the probability of employment for an individual i in the sample is given by:

(1) $$P_i = \int_{-\infty}^{\beta'X_i} \frac{1}{(2\pi)^{1/2}} \exp(-t^2/2) dt$$

with:

(2) $$\beta'X_i = \beta_o + \beta_1 MALE_i + \beta_2 EDUC_i + \beta_3 EXPER_i + \beta_4 CLT15_i + \beta_5 HOH_i + \beta_6 FORPRES_i$$

where the ß$_j$ coefficients are to be estimated and the variable definitions and sample means are as given in Table 1, with the variable MALE equal to one if the person is male, EDUC is years of education, EXPER represents potential years of experience, CLT15 represents number of children less than 15, HOH is equal to one if the person is the head of the household, and FORPRES represents foreign presence in the local labor market, as defined earlier (for discussion of the standard probit model, and its limitations, see Maddala, 1983 and Greene, 1990). The probit equations were estimated using LIMDEP version 6.0 (Greene, 1992).

We present two sets of probit equation estimates in Table 3, one for each of our measures of foreign presence. We also explored a number of other, alternative specifications, including regional variables, the square of experience, and occupational dummies, among others. Our results were remarkably robust, with the estimated coefficients of the variables presented in Table 3 generally differing only in the third decimal place.

Table 3: Probit Results on Determinants of Employment

Probit 1: Foreign Presence Measured by % of Foreigners in Region
Dependent Variable: Employed (= 1 if employed, = 0 if unemployed)

Observations	493
Log-Likelihood	-132.9023
Restricted (Slopes=0) Log-L.	-141.2102
Chi-Squared (6)	16.61586
Significance Level	0.0108037

Probit Results

Variable	Coefficient	Std. Error	t-ratio	Prob|t|_x
Constant	0.10283	0.5629	0.183	0.85505
MALE	0.39891	0.1800	2.217	0.02665
EDUC	0.07247	0.0383	1.891	0.05865
EXPER	0.01108	0.0073	1.521	0.12834
CLT15	0.27593	0.1486	1.856	0.06340
HOH	-0.40396	0.2073	-1.949	0.05131
FORPRES	0.03384	0.0337	1.004	0.31550

Variable Estimates of the Marginal Effects of X

	Coefficient	Std. Error	t-ratio	Prob|t|_x
Constant	0.01392	0.0764	0.182	0.85544
MALE	0.05399	0.0241	2.238	0.02525
EDUC	0.00981	0.0051	1.931	0.05345
EXPER	0.00150	0.0010	1.533	0.12523
CLT15	0.03735	0.0194	1.925	0.05427
HOH	0.05468	0.0281	-1.948	0.05144
FORPRES	0.00458	0.0046	1.004	0.31519

Table 3 continued

Probit 2: Foreign Presence Measured by Survey Question on #s in Neighborhood

Dependent Variable: Employed (= 1 if employed, = 0 if unemployed)

Observations	493
Log-Likelihood	-131.8431
Restricted (Slopes=0) Log-L.	-141.2102
Chi-Squared (7)	18.73417
Significance Level	0.0090621

Probit Results

Variable	Coefficient	Std. Error	t-ratio	Prob|t|_x
Constant	0.48352	0.5143	0.940	0.34711
MALE	0.39478	0.1809	2.183	0.02904
EDUC	0.07337	0.0387	1.898	0.05769
EXPER	0.01133	0.0074	1.540	0.12351
CLT15	0.25081	0.1500	1.672	0.09457
HOH	-0.40398	0.2094	-1.929	0.05374
MANY	-0.53766	0.2971	-1.810	0.07031
FEW	-0.12019	0.1884	-0.638	0.52346

Variable Estimates of the Marginal Effects of X

	Coefficient	Std. Error	t-ratio	Prob|t|_x
Constant	0.06447	0.0696	0.927	0.35411
MALE	0.05264	0.0239	2.201	0.02775
EDUC	0.00978	0.0050	1.941	0.05221
EXPER	0.00151	0.0010	1.554	0.12019
CLT15	0.03344	0.0194	1.726	0.08439
HOH	-0.05387	0.0279	-1.932	0.05330
MANY	-0.07169	0.0396	-1.812	0.06996
FEW	-0.01603	0.0250	-0.640	0.52221

Note: MANY = 1 if many foreigners in neighborhood, FEW = 1 if few foreigners in neighborhood, NONE in neighborhood is the dummy variable left out of the equation; CLT15 = number of children less than 15 in household; HOH = 1 if head of household; EXPER = potential experience in years (age - age left school - 6); EDUC = education in years (age left school - 6); MALE = 1 if respondent is male; FORPRES = % of foreigners living in region.

Source: Our Calculations from the data (Reif and Melich, 1991).

From Table 3 we see that being male affects the probability of being employed positively. Also affecting employment positively at the .10 significance level is education and number of children less than 15, while at the .13 significance level, experience adds to the probability of being employed. The anomaly in terms of our expectations is the head of household status variable (HOH), which has a negative coefficient indicating that the probability of employment is lower for heads of household. As we discussed earlier, this may be a result of the sampling process: unemployed heads of household are more likely to be home and available to respond to the survey.

The striking result of the estimated equations involves the link between the presence of foreigners and the probability of being employed. Using our objective measure of foreign presence - the percentage of foreigners in the region - probit equation (1) in Table 3 shows that there is no statistically significant link between this variable and the likelihood of employment among German residents. Foreign presence does not appear to reduce the probability of employment at the individual level and, in fact, seems to increase it (although the positive connection is not statistically significant by conventional standards). Using the more subjective measure of foreign presence - respondents' perception of the number of foreigners living in their neighborhood - we do find that people living in neighborhoods with many foreigners are more likely to be unemployed (at the .07 significance level). This again *could* be a result of the unemployed mis-perceiving the number of unemployed in their neighborhoods, or that they live in neighborhoods with more foreigners.[14] However, it may also be that this more localized measure of foreign presence better captures the labor market influence of foreigners. In the latter case, our results provide some weak evidence that foreign presence raises the probability of unemployment.

---

[14] Also, this measure of foreigner may include ethnic Germans, since it is a self-definition and not an official one.

4 European Attitudes Toward Foreigners

The Eurobarometer survey contains a wealth of information on attitudes toward foreigners, which we only begin to draw on here and in the next section. In this section, we examine attitudes toward foreigners in various European countries by looking at some tabulations of their responses to questions about foreigners in general (Table 4) and particular groups of foreigners (Table 5). In the next section we perform a more disaggregated analysis of how attitudes vary by labor market status in Germany (Tables 6 and 8). We should emphasize the exploratory nature of this analysis.

Our sample for Europe, drawn from Eurobarometer 30, consists of 10,126 respondents from the twelve EEC nations. As in our analysis of employment effects of foreigners in Germany in the last section, here we look at the opinions of citizens in each country, 16 years of age or older, not of foreign origin and not in the military (thus, a Dutch citizen living in Italy is not included in the sample). Special questions on immigrants were asked by the Eurobarometer survey of citizens in France, Netherlands, Germany and the United Kingdom. Table 4 presents the responses of citizens from these nations and from the EEC as a whole (thus including also Belgium, Denmark, Greece, Ireland, Italy, Luxembourg, Portugal and Spain).

As background information, the first two rows of Table 4 exhibit the percentage of the population that consists of foreigners in each country and the EEC (note that the data shows that Germany has a proportion of foreigners, 7.3%, which is about twice the EEC average, 3.6%). The rest of Table 4 depicts the opinions that citizens in the various countries and the overall EEC have about various issues relating to foreigners and immigration. We first report the opinions that persons have about all foreigners, where the latter include not only persons born outside the EEC but also persons born inside the EEC who have migrated to other countries (such as Southern Europeans in Germany). In the last row of Table 4 we then depict the opinions expressed specifically about non-EEC nationals.

The responses to each opinion question should be read in the following way: 1) rows depict responses to particular questions, 2) the numbers in each box represent the decomposition of the column group according to the various responses in the row. For example, let us examine the third column, which gives the opinions of citizens in France. Consider the tenth row in Table 4, which corresponds to an opinion question asking individuals their attitude toward the single European market in Europe. The percentages in the corresponding box show that 6.6% of the French think that a single European market is bad, 45.0% are indifferent, 43.3% think it is good, and 5.1% don't know or didn't answer. The respective percentages for the overall EEC sample are 7.7%, 26.5%, 55.0% and 10.8%. The same exercise can be performed for each question in Table 4's rows according to the country depicted in the Table's columns.

Table 4: Attitudes Towards Foreigners for Various European Countries

Variables	Response	France	Netherlands	Germany	United Kingdom	Europe (12 EEC nations)
% foreigners in population*		5.0	3.8	7.3	3.0	3.6
Sample size		564	740	858	1031	10,126

Opinions about All Foreigners, including Other EEC Nationals
(column percentage for each question)

Variables	Response	France	Netherlands	Germany	United Kingdom	Europe (12 EEC nations)
Foreigners in our country	too many	47.9	32.8	47.4	36.1	29.8
	a lot	43.8	50.1	44.8	36.6	39.4
	not many	6.0	11.6	6.9	24.3	25.0
	dk/na	2.3	5.4	0.9	3.0	5.9
Foreigners presence disturbing	yes	14.4	8.9	16.9	8.5	9.8
	no	82.3	86.1	78.3	89.3	86.8
	dk/na	3.4	5.0	4.8	2.1	3.3
Foreigners in neighborhood	many	14.5	15.1	7.0	5.2	8.3
	few	38.3	48.1	52.1	49.4	42.2
	none	47.2	36.8	40.9	45.7	49.5
Foreigners children in schools lowers the level of education	yes	29.8	28.9	25.2	23.8	19.9
	no	70.2	71.1	74.8	76.2	80.1
Foreigners increase our unemployment	yes	35.8	26.6	29.0	32.6	32.3
	no	64.2	73.4	71.0	67.4	67.7
A single market in Europe is good	bad	6.6	6.1	7.9	12.6	7.7
	indifferent	45.0	35.8	36.6	27.3	26.5
	good	43.3	47.7	45.6	48.9	55.0
	dk/na	5.1	10.4	9.9	11.3	10.8

Opinions about Non-EEC Nationals
(column percentage for each question)

Variables	Response	France	Netherlands	Germany	United Kingdom	Europe (12 EEC nations)
Is their presence good or bad for the future of our country?	bad	17.9	8.4	14.7	10.1	9.6
	little bad	30.7	19.3	28.0	21.5	22.2
	little good	30.1	50.9	31.4	40.6	33.3
	good	9.4	10.7	7.7	9.9	13.5
	dk/na	11.9	10.7	18.3	17.8	21.5

*Percentage of foreigners in actual population in 1989; from Zimmermann (1991).
dk/na = don't know/did not answer.
Numbers may not add to 100% because of rounding.
Source: Our calculations from the data [Reif and Melich (1991)].

The first opinion question reported in Table 4 involves whether individuals felt that foreigners in their country were: too many, a lot, or not many (with the category dk/na representing no answers or did not know). The responses show the variety of perceptions in Europe, with those countries with higher proportions of foreigners in the population having a greater proportion of citizens who feel that there are too many foreigners. Note that, compared to some countries with lower amounts of immigration - such as France - Germany has a lower proportion of the population whose perception is that there are too many foreigners. This result also appears in the responses to some other questions reported in Table 4. For instance, one question asked respondents whether "foreigners increase our unemployment." In Germany, the proportion of respondents answering "no" to this question was 71% while in the EEC overall the corresponding proportion was 67.7%, with France having a response of 64.2%. Clearly, the attitude of German residents toward the possible unemployment effects of foreigners is less negative than in the EEC overall, in spite of the much larger inflows of foreign workers into that country. This, however, only provides us with the views of the overall German citizen population, not particular groups, such as the unemployed, or younger workers. The next section will deal with that particular topic.

In Table 5 we look at the opinions of citizens in various countries and the EEC overall toward various specific groups of "foreigners," including Southern Europeans, North Africans, Turks, Black Africans, Asians, South-East Asians, West Indians, Jews, Surinamers and Northern European. The question asked individuals whether they "disliked, liked or were indifferent to" members of these particular groups. As with our analysis of Table 4, we find that the relative dislike for foreigners in a particular country is correlated with the proportion of the population consisting of foreigners in that country. The Netherlands and the United Kingdom, with the smaller fraction of foreigners in the population, also display the lowest "dislike" toward foreigners. However, the relative "like" or "dislike" of foreigners varies by foreign group and by country. In France, for instance, 33.9% of the population said that they disliked North Africans, but only 9.2% said they disliked West Indians and only 4.8% disliked Northern Europeans. By comparison, in Germany 22.7% of the citizens surveyed said that they disliked North Africans, 18.4% said they disliked West Indians and 4.7% disliked Northern Europeans. Considering the larger relative proportion of foreigners in the population, German citizens do not appear to exhibit greater "dislike" of foreigners than other countries (if one takes a comparison with France, which has a lower proportion of foreigners, Germany has a greater portion of the population who "like" Southern Europeans, North Africans, Turks and Northern Europeans). Different groups within Germany, however, may have varying opinions on these immigrants. The purpose of the next section is to examine this question.

Table 5: Attitudes Towards Particular Groups for Various European Countries (column percentage for each question)

Variables	Response	France	Netherlands	Germany	United Kingdom
Sample Size		564	740	858	1031
Southern Europeans	dislike	5.0	3.1	9.1	4.3
	indifferent	56.0	63.5	49.9	45.7
	like	39.0	33.4	41.0	50.0
North Africans	dislike	33.9	8.9	22.7	12.4
	indifferent	52.0	70.4	59.4	51.2
	like	14.2	20.7	17.8	36.4
Turks	dislike	32.8	11.7	27.5	12.2
	indifferent	53.7	66.2	54.3	52.8
	like	13.5	22.3	18.2	35.0
Black Africans	dislike	20.7	8.1	26.3	12.4
	indifferent	61.7	69.3	55.9	48.9
	like	17.6	22.6	17.7	38.7
Asians	dislike	24.6	7.7	32.8	16.4
	indifferent	59.6	69.9	53.5	45.2
	like	15.8	22.4	13.8	38.4
South-East Asians	dislike	20.4	7.3	25.4	12.8
	indifferent	58.0	69.3	56.1	49.6
	like	21.6	23.4	18.5	37.6
West Indians	dislike	9.2	7.2	18.4	12.6
	indifferent	53.7	64.1	60.0	47.1
	like	37.1	28.8	21.6	40.3
Jews	dislike	13.3	1.9	15.2	5.5
	indifferent	55.3	54.7	58.4	45.5
	like	31.4	43.4	26.5	49.0
Surinamers	dislike		8.9		
	indifferent		64.3		
	like		26.8		
Northern Europeans	dislike	4.8	1.6	4.7	3.0
	indifferent	47.9	55.0	37.3	39.4
	like	47.3	43.4	58.0	57.6

Numbers may not add to 100% because of rounding.
We recoded the responses in the Eurobarometer survey in the following manner Dislike = 1-4, Indifferent = 0 or 5-7, Like = 7-10.
Source: Our calculations from the data [Reif and Melich (1991)].

5 German Attitudes Toward Foreigners and Their Determinants

In this section we disaggregate, for Germany, the responses of Tables 4 and 5 by labor market status. This allows us to get some idea of the correlation between an individual's position in the labor market and attitudes toward different groups of foreigners. Our approach is to first look at some cross-tabulations of different measures of attitudes toward foreigners by employment status (Table 6). Second, we examine the determinants of attitudes more formally, using a probit equation estimating the role played by various factors in explaining the attitudes of German residents toward foreigners (Table 8). Analyzing the determinants of attitudes in this manner permits us to examine the impact of a particular variable - such as employment status - holding constant other factors. It also allows us to examine the statistical significance of our results. Recall that our data consists of the subgroup of 858 German citizens 16 years of age or older, not of foreign origin and not in the military. Our analysis is only relevant to the extent that the attitudes of these respondents are "representative" of the attitudes found in the general public.

Table 6 is read in the same way as Tables 4 and 5. The first group we look at in Table 6 includes all foreigners, including EEC nationals. We then report German opinions about foreigners excluding EEC nationals. We follow with attitudes toward particular groups of foreigners. Finally, we depict some more specific opinions asked of German respondents in the sample, including attitudes toward the presence of Turks in Germany. The figures in Table 6 exhibit the wide variation of attitudes toward foreigners by labor force status in Germany.

Table 6: German Attitudes Towards Foreigners Broken Down by Employment Status

Variables	Response	Employed	Unemployed	Student	Out of the Labor Force	Retired	Total
Sample size		452	41	69	129	167	858
Opinions about All Foreigners, including Other EEC Nationals (column percentage for each question)							
Foreigners in our country	too many	47.4	41.5	20.3	51.2	57.5	47.4
	a lot	43.8	48.8	66.7	44.2	37.7	44.8
	not many	7.7	9.8	13.0	4.7	3.0	6.9
	dk/na	1.1	0.0	0.0	0.0	1.8	0.9
Foreigners presence disturbing	yes	16.4	14.6	8.7	14.0	24.6	16.9
	no	78.3	78.1	84.1	83.0	72.5	78.3
	dk/na	5.3	7.3	7.25	3.1	3.0	4.8
Foreigners in neighborhood	many	6.4	14.6	7.3	4.7	8.4	7.0
	few	54.7	56.1	63.8	45.7	44.3	52.1
	none	38.9	29.3	29.0	49.6	47.3	40.9
Foreigner's children in schools lowers the level of education	yes	24.5	26.8	20.3	30.2	24.6	25.2
	no	75.4	73.2	79.7	69.8	75.5	74.8
Foreigners increase our unemployment	yes	27.0	26.8	17.4	33.3	36.5	29.0
	no	73.0	73.2	82.6	66.7	63.5	71.0
A single market in Europe is good	bad	7.7	7.3	4.35	6.2	11.4	7.9
	indifferent	35.6	19.5	33.3	40.3	41.9	36.6
	good	46.2	58.5	62.3	44.7	34.1	45.6
	dk/na	10.4	14.6	0.0	8.5	12.8	9.9

Table 6 continued

Variables	Response	Employed	Unemployed	Student	Out of the Labor Force	Retired	Total
Opinions about Non-EEC Nationals (column percentage for each question)							
Is their presence is good or bad for the future of Germany	bad	14.6	9.8	4.4	12.4	22.2	14.7
	little bad	28.1	17.1	18.8	30.2	32.3	28.0
	little good	31.2	36.6	49.3	29.5	24.6	31.4
	good	7.5	9.8	14.5	8.5	4.2	7.7
	dk/na	18.6	26.8	13.1	19.4	16.8	18.3
Opinions on Particular Groups (column percentage for each question)							
Southern Europeans	dislike	7.1	12.2	7.3	7.0	16.2	9.1
	indifferent	48.5	53.7	27.5	60.5	53.9	49.9
	like	44.5	34.2	65.2	32.6	29.94	41.0
North Africans	dislike	19.0	31.7	8.7	23.3	35.9	22.7
	indifferent	62.4	56.1	56.5	60.5	52.7	59.4
	like	18.6	12.2	34.8	16.3	11.4	17.8
Turks	dislike	24.6	36.6	17.4	28.7	36.5	27.5
	indifferent	55.5	41.5	56.5	55.8	52.1	54.3
	like	19.9	22.0	26.1	15.5	11.4	18.2
Black Africans	dislike	22.1	29.3	10.1	30.2	40.7	26.3
	indifferent	59.1	53.7	50.7	56.6	49.7	55.9
	like	18.8	17.1	39.1	13.2	9.6	17.7
Asians	dislike	29.9	31.7	11.6	40.3	43.7	32.8
	indifferent	56.2	51.2	58.0	51.2	46.7	53.5
	like	13.9	17.1	30.4	8.5	9.6	13.8

Table 6 continued

Variables	Response	Employed	Unemployed	Student	Out of the Labor Force	Retired	Total
South-East Asians	dislike	21.7	29.3	7.3	30.2	38.3	25.4
	indifferent	59.5	48.8	53.6	58.9	47.3	56.1
	like	18.8	21.2	39.1	10.9	14.4	18.5
West Indians	dislike	15.3	24.4	2.9	20.2	30.5	18.4
	indifferent	61.1	56.1	52.2	65.1	57.5	60.0
	like	23.7	19.5	44.9	14.7	12.0	21.6
Jews	dislike	12.2	24.4	2.9	17.8	24.0	15.2
	indifferent	59.5	53.7	52.2	62.8	55.7	58.4
	like	28.2	22.0	44.9	19.4	20.4	26.5
Northern Europeans	dislike	4.7	9.8	4.4	3.9	4.2	4.7
	indifferent	37.6	41.5	23.2	47.3	33.6	37.3
	like	57.7	48.8	72.5	48.8	62.3	58.0
Questions about Turks (column percentage for each question)							
Turks take our jobs	disagree	52.8	46.3	75.4	46.5	43.1	51.5
	agree	32.7	51.2	21.7	46.5	50.9	43.5
	dk/na	4.4	2.4	2.9	7.0	6.0	4.9
We should send back all non- economically active Turks	yes	19.3	24.4	8.7	22.5	21.0	19.5
	no	80.8	75.6	91.3	77.5	79.0	80.5

Numbers many not add to 100% because of rounding. For the variables on "opinions on particular groups", we recoded the responses in the following manner Dislike = 1-4, Indifferent = 0 or 5-7, Like = 7-10. dk/na = don't know/did not answer. Source: Our calculations from the data (Reif and Melich, 1991).

The cross-tabulations in Table 6 indicate that most of the resident population in Germany thinks that there are a large number of foreigners living in their country. Almost half of the sample believes that there are too many foreigners (compared to 47.9% in France, 32.8% in Netherlands, and 36.1% in the United Kingdom, see Table 4). This attitude is less severe among students, and, surprisingly, less strong among the unemployed when compared to the employed. In spite of the fact that many Germans think there are too many foreigners in the country, a much smaller proportion, 16.9%, finds their presence disturbing. Again, students find foreigners less disturbing and retirees find them more disturbing. Going across the various rows in Table 6, we see that 42.7% of the respondents in the sample think that the presence of non-EEC foreigners in the country is not good for the future of Germany. As before, the variation in responses follows a consistent pattern across employment status, with students at the very low end of negativism, retirees at the top, and the unemployed having less stringent attitudes toward foreigners than the employed.

The attitudes just discussed are toward a generic "foreigner." The survey also examined attitudes toward particular groups of foreigners. Table 6 shows that less than 10% of the respondents disliked Southern Europeans and Northern Europeans. However, compared to the employed, twice as many of the unemployed disliked these groups. This ratio also holds for attitudes toward Jews, and the pattern holds also for North Africans, Turks, Black Africans, South-East Asians and West Indians. The most disliked group by persons in the sample are Asians - 32.8% of the overall German population sampled disliked this group - and the negative attitude is about equal among the employed and unemployed.

One of the strongest anti-foreigner responses arose in response to the question "do foreigners' children in schools lower the level of education?". While there is not much variation across employment status, Table 6 shows that fully 25% of the sample responded yes to this question (comparable to respondents in other European nations, see Table 4). We pursued further the attitudes of German residents toward the children of immigrants by disaggregating the responses according to the number of children present in the household. The results are presented in Table 7, which (though the number of cases is small) displays a pattern: the larger the number of children in the household, the more likely that the respondent thinks that foreign children in schools lower the level of education. From an economic perspective, this result seems to suggest that the native-born have a strong fear that foreigners will lower the educational levels of their children, thus reducing the returns to their investments on those children. Alternatively, one could postulate that a third variable, such as respondent education or age, may be involved.[15]

---

[15] Editor Gunter Steinmann suggests the responses on school education largely depend on the definition of region and type of school. A gymnasium is not affected by the low percentage of foreign students; but Hauptschule's in urban districts often have more than 80% foreign students, making teaching in German

Table 7: Number of Children and Attitude Towards Foreigners in German Schools (percentage of respondents in column with yes or no response)

foreigners children in schools lowers the level of education	no children under 15 in household	one child under 15 in household	two children under 15 in household	three children under 15 in household	four children under 15 in household	Total
No	76.2	76.2	63.4	64.3	50.0	74.8
Yes	23.8	23.9	36.6	35.7	50.0	25.2
Total number of respondents	660	109	71	14	4	858

Source: Our calculations from the data Reif and Melich (1991).

To explore the role of a particular variable in influencing the probability that a person will take on a particular attitude, holding other things equal, we carried out a multivariate probit analysis specifying how a set of explanatory variables determines the probability of a person taking a particular attitude toward foreigners. We report these results in Table 8. Note that this analysis allows us to determine if a particular variable, such as employment status, is significant in explaining attitudes, other variables held constant.

We estimate the probit equations on the German data in two ways. First, we run a probit equation on the sample including all labor force states. Second, we carry out a probit analysis on a sample including only those in the labor force (the employed and unemployed). This allows us to compare and link the present results with our earlier discussion relating employment status and foreign presence in local labor markets. For each sample examined, we carry out our probit analysis using three dependent variables, which reflect the responses to three different questions involving foreigners. The three questions are: (1) whether the children of foreigners lowers the level of education, (2) whether foreigners increase our unemployment, and (3) whether foreigners' presence is bad for the future of germany.

Table 8 reports the results of the six probit equations we carried out. The explanatory variables reported in Table 8 include the labor status variables: EMPSTAT2 (whether the person was unemployed), EMPSTAT3 (whether the person was a student), EMPSTAT4 (whether the person was out of the labor force), and EMPSTAT5 (whether the person was retired), plus the previously-defined variables: MALE, EDUC, EXPER, CLT15, HOH and FORPRES, MANY and FEW.

---

difficult. The responses on the effect of foreigners on childrens' education thus depend on the location, characteristics, etc. of those interviewed. This point is worth noting and, again, the generality of our results depends on how representative the Eurobarometer sample is of Germany's population.

In examining the determinants of the responses to the question as to whether the children of foreigners lower the level of education, the set of explanatory variables used in the analysis were jointly statistically insignificant in explaining the probability of answering yes to this question. Still, education was significant in these probit equations (at a .1 level), with a negative sign. Employment status was insignificant, but the number of children less than 15 in the household was significant (generally at the .05 level) and positive, confirming the picture obtained from the cross-tabulations in Table 7.

Moving on, we examine the determinants of attitudes involving the questions as to whether "foreigners increase our unemployment", and whether "foreigners' presence is bad for the future of Germany". The multivariate analysis displayed in Table 8 confirms our earlier cross-tabulations. We noted before, for instance, that in response to the question "is the presence of foreigners good or bad for the future of Germany," a total of 42.7% of the employed said it is bad or a little bad, while only 26.9% of the unemployed answered thus. These results hold up in the multivariate analysis carried out in the probit equations. In Table 8 we see that unemployment status is statistically significant and negative in sign - indicating the unemployed are more likely than the employed to feel that the presence of foreigners is good for the future of Germany. This is true after holding education and experience constant.

Finally, let us consider what the probit coefficients tell us about the responses to two questions directly related to labor market status: "foreigners increase our unemployment" and "Turks take our jobs." Using cross-tabulations, we find that overall, 43.5% of the German population sampled thinks that Turks take jobs from them, and broken down by employment status we see that 32.7% of the employed versus 51.2% of the unemployed think Turks take jobs away. On the other hand, the response of the typical German resident to the question of whether a generic foreigner increases German unemployment is mostly "no," but the numbers saying "yes" are not negligible: 29.0% of the overall sample, 27.0% of the employed and 26.8% of the unemployed. These results are confirmed by the probit equations shown in Table 8, in which the variables EMPSTAT and FORPRES are insignificant in determining attitudes toward immigrants.

Unemployment and Attitudes Towards Foreigners in Germany 147

Table 8: Probit Results on Determinants of Attitudes in Germany

I. Results from Entire Sample

Probit 1: Dependent variable is "foreigners' children in schools lowers the level of education"

Variable	Coefficient	t-ratio	Coefficient	t-ratio
Constant	-0.32306	-0.963	-0.48358	-1.611
EMPSTAT2	0.06918	0.311	0.05443	0.244
EMPSTAT3	0.27440	1.188	0.26666	1.152
EMPSTAT4	0.01593	0.100	0.02765	0.173
EMPSTAT5	-0.12072	-0.706	-0.11062	-0.647
MALE	-0.09117	-0.839	-0.08224	-0.755
EDUC	-0.04139	-1.925	-0.04060	-1.884
EXPER	0.003796	0.878	0.00418	0.971
CLT15	0.16281	2.486	0.17268	2.624
HOH	0.09064	0.760	0.07320	0.616
FORPRES	-0.00954	-0.480		
MANY			0.26231	1.417
FEW			0.09432	0.945
Observations	858		858	
Log-Likelihood	-476.4227		-475.4015	
Slopes=0 Log-L.	-484.1245		-484.1245	
Chi-Squared (10)	15.4037		17.4460	
Significance Level	0.118		0.095	

Probit 2: Dependent variable is "foreigners increase our unemployment"

Variable	Coefficient	t-ratio	Coefficient	t-ratio
Constant	0.29772	0.897	0.30736	1.047
EMPSTAT2	-0.04719	-0.210	-0.05194	-0.231
EMPSTAT3	0.23046	0.975	0.23001	0.973
EMPSTAT4	0.03039	0.193	0.03101	0.197
EMPSTAT5	0.18116	1.091	0.17677	1.064
MALE	0.01288	0.121	0.00115	0.108
EDUC	-0.08626	-4.002	-0.08552	-3.968
EXPER	0.00987	0.234	0.00090	0.214
CLT15	0.07692	1.167	0.07509	1.139
HOH	-0.01959	-0.167	-0.01634	-0.140
FORPRES	-0.00109	-0.056		
MANY			0.06924	0.374
FEW			-0.05586	-0.576
Observations	858		858	
Log-Likelihood	-501.0943		-500.7703	
Slopes=0 Log-L.	-516.8072		-516.8072	
Chi-Squared (10)	31.4259		32.0738	
Significance Level	0.000		0.001	

Probit 3: Dependent variable is "foreigners presence is bad for the future of Germany"

Variable	Coefficient	t-ratio	Coefficient	t-ratio
Constant	0.22755	0.735	0.36827	1.332
EMPSTAT2	-0.48193	-2.132	-0.49911	-2.196
EMPSTAT3	0.07241	0.332	0.06525	0.299
EMPSTAT4	-0.20579	-1.360	-0.21007	-1.387
EMPSTAT5	-0.07691	-0.483	-0.08871	-0.557
MALE	0.03474	0.341	0.03073	0.301
EDUC	-0.06827	-3.450	-0.06774	-3.418
EXPER	0.01087	2.698	0.01046	2.605
CLT15	0.02277	0.360	0.01577	0.249
HOH	-0.01150	-0.103	0.00160	0.014
FORPRES	0.01252	0.683		
MANY			0.08384	0.468
FEW			-0.08802	-0.948
Observations	858		858	
Log-Likelihood	-558.4329		-557.9138	
Slopes=0 Log-L.	-585.4350		-585.4350	
Chi-Squared (10)	54.0042		55.0423	
Significance Level	0.0000		0.000	

II. Results from Those in the Labor Force

Probit 1: Dependent variable is "foreigners' children in schools lowers the level of education"

Variable	Coefficient	t-ratio	Coefficient	t-ratio
Constant	-0.08806	-0.203	-0.40485	-1.014
EMP	-0.07839	-0.350	-0.04908	-0.218
MALE	-0.00897	-0.064	0.00758	0.054
EDUC	-0.04653	-1.787	-0.04789	-1.827
EXPER	0.00384	0.724	0.00408	0.765
CLT15	0.15500	1.972	0.18118	2.288
HOH	0.00556	0.036	-0.00959	-0.062
FORPRES	-0.02025	-0.778		
MANY			0.50125	2.077
FEW			0.16228	1.206
Observations	493		493	
Log-Likelihood	-271.2288		-269.2552	
Slopes=0 Log-L.	-275.8495		-275.8495	
Chi-Squared (7)	9.2414		13.1885	
Significance Level	0.236		0.1055	

Probit 2: Dependent variable is "foreigners increase our unemployment"

Variable	Coefficient	t-ratio	Coefficient	t-ratio
Constant	0.53829	1.232	0.57639	1.451
EMP	0.04148	0.184	0.03918	0.174
MALE	0.07036	0.505	0.06308	0.452
EDUC	-0.10320	-3.867	-0.10126	-3.795
EXPER	-0.00691	-1.310	-0.00706	-1.335
CLT15	0.13479	1.714	0.12906	1.644
HOH	0.00245	0.016	0.01223	0.080
FORPRES	-0.00217	-0.084		
MANY			-0.01311	-0.053
FEW			-0.13186	-1.014
Observations	493		493	
Log-Likelihood	-278.4333		-277.8877	
Slopes=0 Log-L.	-287.4371		-287.4371	
Chi-Squared (7)	18.0076		19.0989	
Significance Level	0.012		0.014	

Probit 3: Dependent variable is "foreigners presence is bad for the future of Germany"

Variable	Coefficient	t-ratio	Coefficient	t-ratio
Constant	-0.36566	-0.887	-0.25150	-0.665
EMP	0.46967	2.051	0.47512	2.063
MALE	0.13932	1.046	0.13135	0.984
EDUC	-0.06151	-2.562	-0.06034	-2.510
EXPER	0.01598	3.214	0.01585	3.187
CLT15	-0.03226	-0.420	-0.04278	-0.554
HOH	-0.09558	-0.654	-0.08326	-0.573
FORPRES	0.00779	0.325		
MANY			-0.03493	-0.147
FEW			-0.12036	-0.976
Observations	493		493	
Log-Likelihood	-319.2051		-318.7692	
Slopes=0 Log-L.	-334.3572		-334.3572	
Chi-Squared (7)	30.3042		31.1761	
Significance Level	0.000		0.000	

Note: Dependent variable = 1 if attitude, 0 otherwise; PRESENCE = 1 if response was bad or bad to some extent, 0 otherwise; EMP =1 if employed, 0 if unemployed; EMPSTAT2 = 1 if unemployed; EMPSTAT3 = 1 if student; EMPSTAT4 = 1 if out of the labor force; EMPSTAT5 = 1 if retiree; EMPSTAT1 = employed is the omitted dummy variable; MANY = 1 if many foreigners in neighborhood, FEW = 1 if few foreigners in neighborhood, NONE in neighborhood is the dummy variable left out of the equation; CLT15 = number of children less than 15 in household; HOH = 1 if head of household; EXPER = potential experience in years (age - age left school - 6); EDUC = education in years (age left school - 6); MALE = 1 if respondent is male; FORPRES = % of foreigners living in region.
Source: Our calculations from the data (Reif and Melich, 1991).

6 Synthesis and Conclusions

This paper deals with two questions relevant to the economic consequences of immigration to Germany: (1) does the presence of foreigners affect labor market status? and (2) does labor market status determine attitudes toward foreigners?. For the latter, we specifically ask if the unemployed and employed feel differently about foreigners, and whether persons in other labor market categories diverge from these groups in their opinions.

With respect to question (1), our results indicate that the presence of foreigners in a labor market is not significantly associated with the likelihood of a German resident being unemployed. That being said, we do find some weak evidence that Germans located in neighborhoods where they believe many foreigners are present have a lower probability of employment. There is, however, a difficulty in interpreting this latter result because the measure of foreign presence is self-reported by the respondents. Self-reported presence means that, when asked about the number of foreigners in their neighborhood, the unemployed responded "many" much more often than other groups. We are left to ponder whether the unemployed live in neighborhoods where many foreigners live, which may thus lead to greater job competition with the foreigners, or whether the unemployed just mistakenly perceive that there are too many foreigners in their neighborhood.

Our results on the determinants of German attitudes toward foreigners are mixed. Generally, students have the most positive attitudes toward foreigners and retirees the most negative. On several of the attitude questions that we analyzed using the Eurobarometer data there was relatively little variation by employment status. We do find, though, that when the survey's opinion questions shifted from asking attitudes about "generic" foreigners to seeking opinions about specific groups, the unemployed generally surfaced as having a greater likelihood of "dislike" toward foreigners when compared to the employed.

The fact that negative reactions toward foreigners based on labor market status are not generally focussed on foreigners in general but toward particular groups of foreigners (Turks but not Southern Europeans, for instance), could be taken to imply that non-economic variables linked to prejudice and discrimination - toward those particular groups-may lie behind the attitudes. Alternatively, it could suggest that analyses of the impact of foreigners on the employment of the native-born should take into account differences in the characteristics of the immigrant groups (skills, demographic characteristics) in determining the effects of the foreigners. The employment impact of immigrants on German residents, and the attitudes of Germans toward foreigners in turn could diverge depending on the particular immigrant group being considered and the specific German group being examined or voicing its opinion.

Our analysis has neglected the role of social transfers in attitude formation. If social transfers are important in determining attitudes, this variable may offer an explanation of why in certain cases (eg., the "generic" foreigner) the employed dislike foreigners more that the unemployed do: it may reflect the reluctance of taxpayers compared to nontaxpayers (the unemployed) to finance large social trust bills. This issue goes beyond the bounds of our present paper and our data, but this should be a matter for further research.

We emphasize that, although in this paper we have focused on examining the determinants of German attitudes toward foreigners, a similar analysis could be carried out for other EEC countries. Our own - albeit brief - analysis of EEC attitudes toward foreigners in this paper indicates that "dislike" of foreigners among the citizens of the 12 EEC countries is related to the proportion of foreigners in the economy. On the other hand, attitudes vary by country and by the particular group of foreigners considered (Southern Europeans versus Northern Europeans, for example). In terms of Germany, our analysis of the Eurobarometer's survey opinion responses shows that, compared to some countries with lower amounts of immigration, Germany has a smaller portion of the population whose perception is that there are too many foreigners or that foreigners increase their unemployment.

Finally, some reminders and caveats. The analysis done in this paper was based on 858 respondents to the Eurobarometer survey who are thought to be "representative" of the German population. To the extent that the sample is not "representative", our analysis may lack generality. Moreover, the Eurobarometer data was collected during Fall 1988, before people were actively thinking of unification and long before the numbers of asylum seekers were counted daily in the newspapers. To the extent that recent (and perhaps past) attitudes have been due to perceived or real socio-economic difficulties linked to asylum seekers (such as the expense of social transfers), our analysis is inadequate. However, to the extent that we would expect the unemployed to resent foreigners overall more than the employed do, our research sheds some light.

References

Bean, Frank D., B. Lindsay Lowell, and Lowell Taylor, "Undocumented Mexican Immigrants and the Earnings of Other Workers in the United States," Demography 25, February 1988, 35-52.

Beenstock, Michael, "Learning Hebrew and Finding a Job: Econometric Analysis of Immigrant Absorption in Israel," paper presented at the Centre for Economic Policy Research Workshop on The Economics of International Migration: Econometric Evidence, Konstanz, February 26-27, 1993.

Beggs, J.J. and B.J. Chapman, "Search Efficiency, Skill Transferability and Immigrant Relative Unemployment Rates in Australia," Applied Economics, 22 (2): 249-260, 1990.

Borjas, George J., "The Substitutability of Black, Hispanic, and White Labor," Economic Inquiry 21, 93-106, 1983.

Borjas, George J., "Assimilation, Changes in Cohort Quality, and the Earnings of Immigrants," Journal of Labor Economics, 3, 463-489, 1985.

Borjas, George J., "The Demographic Determinants of the Demand for Black Labor," in The Black Youth Employment Crisis. Edited by R. Freeman and H. Holzer, 191-230. Chicago: University of Chicago Press, 1986.

Borjas, George J., Friends or Strangers: The Impact of Immigrants on the U.S. Economy, New York: Basic Books, 1990.

Card, David, "The Impact of the Mariel Boatlift on the Miami Labor Market," Industrial and Labor Relations Review 43, 1990, 245-257.

Chiswick, Barry R., "The Effect of Americanization on the Earnings of the Foreign-Born," Journal of Political Economy, 86, 897-921, 1978.

Chiswick, Barry R., The Employment of Immigrants in the United States. American Enterprise Institute, Washington D.C., 1982.

Chiswick, Barry R., "The Endogeneity Between Language and Earnings: An International Analysis," paper presented at the Centre for Economic Policy Research Workshop on The Economics of International Migration: Econometric Evidence, Konstanz, February 26-27, 1993.

DeNew, John P. and Klaus F. Zimmermann, "Native Wage Impacts of Foreign Labor: A Random Effects Panel Analysis," Journal of Population Economics, forthcoming, 1994.

Dustmann, Christian, "Speaking Fluency, Writing Fluency and Earnings of Migrants," paper presented at the Centre for Economic Policy Research Conference on The Economics of International Migration: Econometric Evidence, Konstanz, Germany, February 26-27, 1993.

Dutta, Bhaskar, Ira N. Gang and Shubhashis Gangopadhyay, "Subsidy Policies with Capital Accumulation: Maintaining Employment Levels," Journal of Population Economics 2, 1989, 301-318.

Eurostat, Statistical Office of the European Communities, Demographic Statistics, Luxembourg, Eurostat, 1991.

Filer, Randall, "The Effect of Immigrant Arrivals on Migratory Patterns of Native Workers," in John Abowd and Richard Freeman, eds., Immigration, Trade, and the Labor Market Chicago: University of Chicago Press, 1991, 245-270.

Franz, Wolfgang, Ursula Oser and Peter Winker, "Back to the Past and Forward to the Future: Migratory Movements of Guestworkers and Return Emigrants in a Disequilibrium Macroeconometric Model for Germany," paper presented at the Centre for Economic Policy Research Conference on the Economics of International Migration: Econometric Evidence, Konstanz, Germany, February 26-27, 1993.

Gang, Ira N. and Francisco L. Rivera-Batiz, "The Effects of Immigration on European Residents: An Econometric Analysis," Journal of Population Economics, forthcoming, 1994.

Gang, Ira N. and Edward Tower, "Allocating Jobs Under a Minimum Wage: Queues vs. Lotteries," Economic Record 1990, 186-194.

Gang, Ira N. and Shubhashis Gangopadhyay, "Employment, Output and the Choice of Techniques: The Trade-Offs Revisited," Journal of Development Economics 25, 1987, 321-327.

Gang, Ira N. and Shubhashis Gangopadhyay, "A Note on Optimal Policies in Dual Economies," Quarterly Journal of Economics 100, 1985, 1067-1071.

Greene, William H., LIMDEP: User's Manual and Reference Guide: Version 6.0, Bellport, New York: Econometric Software, 1992.

Greene, William H., Econometric Analysis. New York: Macmillan Publishing Company, 1990.

Grossman, Jean Baldwin, "The Substitutability of Natives and Immigrants in Production," Review of Economics and Statistics 64, 1982, 596-603.

Krueger, Alan B. and Jorn Steffen Pischke, "A Comparative Analysis of East and West German Labor markets: Before and After Unification," mimeo., Industrial Relations Section, Princeton University, August 1992.

Lalonde. Robert J. and Robert H. Topel, "The Assimilation of Immigrants in the U.S. Labor market," in George J. Borjas and Richard B. Freeman, eds., Immigration and the Work Force: Economic Consequences for the United States and Source Areas, Chicago: The University of Chicago Press, 1992.

LaLonde, Robert J. and Robert H. Topel, "Labor Market Adjustments to Increased Immigration," in John Abowd and Richard Freeman, eds., Immigration, Trade, and the Labor Market Chicago: University of Chicago Press, 1991.

Layard, Richard, Olivier Blanchard, Rudiger Dornbusch and Paul Krugman, East-West Migration: The Alternatives, The MIT Press, Cambridge, 1992.

Licht, Georg and Viktor Steiner, "Assimilation, Labor Market Experience and Earnings Profiles of Temporary and Permanent Immigrant Workers in Germany," mimeo., 1992.

Maddala, G.S., Limited Dependent and Qualitative Variables in Econometrics, Cambridge: Cambridge University Press, 1983.

Matta, Benjamin and Anthony Popp, "Immigration and the Earnings of Youth in the United States," International Migration Review 22, 1985, 104-116.

Pischke. Jorn-Steffen, "Assimilation and the Earnings of Guestworkers in Germany," mimeo., Zentrun fur Europaische Wirtschaftsforschung, 1992.

Reif, Karlheinz, and Anna Melich. Eurobarometer 30: Immigrants and Out-Groups in Western Europe, October-November 1988 Computer File, Ann Arbor MI: Inter-University Consortium for Political and Social Research Producer and Distributor, 1991.

Rivera-Batiz, Francisco L., "Quantitative Literacy and the Likelihood of Employment among Young Adults," Journal of Human Resources, 27, Spring 1992.

Rivera-Batiz, Francisco L. and Selig L. Sechzer, "Substitution and Complementarity between Immigrant and Native Labor in the United States," in Francisco L. Rivera-Batiz, Selig L. Sechzer and Ira N. Gang, eds., U.S. Immigration Policy Reform in the 1980s: A Preliminary Assessment, New York: Praeger, 1991, 89-116.

Rivera-Batiz, "English Language Proficiency and the Economic Progress of Immigrants," Economics Letters, 34, 295-300, 1990.

Rivera-Batiz, Francisco L., "The Effects of Immigration in a Distorted Two-Sector Economy," Economic Inquiry, 19, October 1981, 626-639.

Schmidt, Christoph, "Country-of-Origin Differences in the Earnings of German Immigrants," University of Munich Discussion Paper No. 92-29, December 1992 (a).

Schmidt, Christoph, "The Earnings Dynamics of Immigrant Labor," University of Munich Discussion Paper No. 92-28, December 1992 (b).

SIBA, Statitiches Jahrbuch, 1991.

Simon, Julian, "Basic Data Concerning Immigration into the United States," The Annals of the American Academy of Political and Social Science, 487, September 1986, 12-56.

TWIG, This Week in Germany, Germany Information Center, New York, 1992.

Ulrich, Ralf, "Economic Behavior of Foreigners in Germany: Some Results from the Socio-Economic Panel," Manuscript, Economics Department, University of Paderborn, Paderborn, Germany, 1991.

Winkelmann, Rainer and Klaus F. Zimmermann, "Ageing, Migration and Labor Mobility," in Paul Johnson and Klaus F. Zimmermann, Labor Market Implications of European Ageing. Cambridge: Cambridge University Press, forthcoming, 1993.

Zimmermann, Klaus F., "Migration Pressure in Germany: Past and Future," Manuscript, SELAPO, Universty of Munich, Germany, 1991.

Vertriebene and *Aussiedler* -
The Immigration of Ethnic Germans[1]

Ralf E. Ulrich
Faculty of Social Sciences
Humboldt University Berlin
Unter den Linden 6
10099 Berlin, Germany

1 Introduction

At the end of the eighties the immigration of ethnic Germans from Eastern Europe to Germany increased sharply. This group constituted a substantial share of the recent immigration wave to Germany. The legal position of the Aussiedler is different from the position of other groups of immigrants, since they are considered to be German citizens. Several public programs have been created to promote the integration of these resettlers.

Immediately after World War II more than 10 million German expellees came to Germany. Their integration is considered as one of the successes of post-war Germany. This experience does influence the German attitude toward the resettlement of Germans from Eastern Europe nowadays. It is also expected that the integration of Aussiedler will be easier than the integration of other groups of immigrants, because of the supposed higher cultural homogeneity. Another argument supporting the optimistic view is the juvenile age structure, the higher labor force participation and the favorable occupational structure of the Aussiedler.

It is general wisdom of immigration theory that the economic impact of immigration depends on structural characteristics of immigrants and on the economic situation of the host country. How similar are today's Aussiedler compared with the German refugees of the late forties? Can we count today on the factors favoring the integration of expellees in the fifties? This paper compares demographic and economic features of Aussiedler and Vertriebene and the general conditions for their integration then and today. The intention is to reach a better understanding of the specific role of Aussiedler currently and in the next years. [2]

---

[1] This paper is based on research supported by the German Research Foundation (DFG).
[2] From the viewpoint of economic history the integration of Vertriebene has been analysed by Schulze/Brelie-Lewien, 1978 and by Kleinert, 1990.

2 The Immigration of German Expellees and Resettlers

Germans from Eastern Europe are the largest group of post-war immigrants on the territory of the Federal Republic of Germany. The magnitude of this immigration and the specific situation after the war required legal regulations to support their integration. Many of the respective laws remained valid for decades. It was only in 1992 that the most important legal act on Aussiedler, the Federal Resettler Law (Bundesvertriebenengesetz), was changed - almost 40 years after it was first passed by the German Parliament.

The legal recognition of a German immigrant as Vertriebener or Aussiedler gave access to certain benefits. For a long time this status also applied to the children of expellees and resettlers, born after the arrival in the FRG. There were different sub-categories of Vertriebene, with different entitlements. The legal definition of these sub-categories was changed several times. Therefore also the statistical definition of Vertriebene and Aussiedler was not constant.

In order to consider the economic impacts of their immigration, three main groups of German immigrants can be distinguished:

- Expellees (*Vertriebene*), who came immediately after the war in a large wave of immigration; their exodus from Eastern Europe was involuntary
- Resettlers (*Aussiedler*), who voluntarily came to Germany after the great expulsion from Eastern Europe,
- Resettlers from East Germany (*Übersiedler*).

The post-war immigration of these groups can be divided into four phases:

- 1944 to 1950: the big wave of involuntary expulsion
- 1951 to 1987: resettlement on a low level
- 1988 to 1990: a rapid increase of resettlement after the liberalization in the East
- after 1991: lower levels of immigration due to a new legal procedure in Germany.

German as well as Soviet authorities already began the resettlement and dispersion of German minorities in the former German territories already in 1940. With the advance of the Red Army this turned into a mass exodus. At the Potsdam Conference the resettlement of German minorities from Poland, Czechoslovakia and the USSR was decided.

Most of the German expellees came in one great wave from 1944 to 1946. The census of October 10, 1946, registered 5.9 million expellees on West German territory (Reichling, 1989, p. 30). Until the beginning of the fifties there was no accurate registration of immigration. The census of March 13, 1950, already counted 7.9 million expellees.[3] Nellner (1959, p. 83) estimated the number of children who inherited the status of an expellee at that time at about 275 thousand. Therefore between 1.5 and 1.7 million expellees must have immigrated to Germany between 1946 and 1950.

During the expulsion most of the Vertriebene left their settlements involuntarily. German historians consider 1949 as the end of expulsion. At that time there was still an estimated number of 4.2 million Germans remaining in Eastern Europe (Reichling, 1986, p. 36).

A substantial part of the remaining Germans also wished also to resettle. During the fifties the hostile climate in their native areas might have been an important factor. With the economic build-up in Germany and the beginning of the cold war there were also other motives for resettlement.

At the end of the forties emigration to Germany was only rarely possible. After the expulsion the communist states of Eastern Europe allowed resettlement only as an exception in cases of "family reunion". On that ticket another 47 thousand resettlers came in 1950, but only 14.8 thousand two years later. In the following 35 years only between 15 and 60 thousand resettlers per year came to Germany. The annual fluctuations reflected temporal changes in the diplomatic relations between the Federal Republic of Germany and the East European countries. Over the whole period from 1950 to 1987 a total of 1.26 million resettlers came to Germany, which is 33 thousand on annual average.

It is obvious that the potential for resettlement was much higher than the actual number of German resettlers. With the liberalization in Eastern Europe at the end of the eighties the number of resettlers soared. 200 thousand Aussiedler came only in 1988, more than three times more than in the previous year. From 1988 to 1991 more than 1.2 million Aussiedler immigrated to Germany. For the first time after the expulsion a substantial share of Aussiedler came from the territory of the former USSR.

After a strong increase from 1988 to 1990, immigration of Aussiedler dropped in 1991 to 220 thousand persons. But this does not reflect a decrease in the emigration potential of Germans in Eastern Europe. The decrease is the result of a change in German legal procedures for the admission of resettlers after July 1, 1990. Before this date, resettlers could apply for the acknowledgment of their German citizenship after arrival in Germany. Under the new regulation the application has to be forwarded from the country of origin. At the same time the criteria for the acknowledgment of German citizenship became more rigid.[4] More time is required to decide on the applications and there is a back congestion of applications. The German Ministry of the Interior reported on more than 500 thousand applications in the process of evaluation at the end of 1991.

---

[3] Because of changing definitions the number of expellees displayed by various census editions are difficult to compare.

[4] The application form contains 53 pages and asks for detailed information even on the grandparents of the applicant and his or her spouse.

How many resettlers should be expected for the next years? This depends on the size of the remaining German minority and their motivation to emigrate.

There are several estimates on the size of the German minority in Eastern Europe. The German Red Cross estimated a total of 3.2 million Germans in Eastern Europe. This includes 1.9 million Germans in the former Soviet Union, 750 thousand in Poland, 62 thousand in Czechoslovakia and 220 thousand in Hungary and Romania each. These estimates relate to persons of German nationality. The number of potential resettlers includes an unknown proportion of non-German spouses.

As with any other kind of migration there are push and pull-factors for the potential German resettlers. When looking at the current economic situation in the East European countries one could expect strong push factors. The transformation toward market economies results in economic and social frictions in its initial stage. Production is still decreasing and unemployment is approaching levels experienced in the Great Recession. The economic gap to Western Europe will widen in the next years. All these factors have generally induced increasing levels of international migration from Eastern to Western Europe in the last years. For the German minorities this economic push factor is supplemented by fears of increasing nationalism in Eastern Europe. Current attempts to redefine the policy against minorities in some countries are not very credible under the current general instability. The pull factors are influenced by the experiences of latest resettlers with their economic and social integration. There should be an effect of chain migration after more than 1.2 million resettlers came to Germany in the last four years. Some of them will prepare the immigration of their relatives who are still in the countries of origin. If the economic situation there deteriorates further older people, who still hesitate to leave their native area, will also come to Germany.

It is uncertain how many of the remaining Germans in Eastern Europe will resettle in Germany. As a high scenario the *Institut der deutschen Wirtschaft* has considered the immigration of all three million Germans until the year 2000, including a proportion of non-German spouses. Moderate estimates expect the resettlement of 60 percent of the German minorities.

3 Demographic and Socioeconomic Characteristics

The effects of immigration and the prospects of integration depend strongly on the characteristics of immigrants. This section compares social and demographic characteristics of the expellees after World War II with today's resettlers.

The age structure of immigrants does influence their labor force participation and their productivity, their effect on old age pension systems and on health insurance systems. Immigrants have generally a juvenile age structure. Most international migration movements come from countries of origin with a higher share of young people to countries with an older age structure. This is intensified by the self-selection of migrants, since the propensity to migrate is stronger among younger age-groups.

The selection effect was not valid for the expellees who came involuntarily to Germany. But the former German territories in Eastern Europe had a younger age structure than West Germany. Therefore the share of younger people was higher among the expellees who immediately came after the war. Chart 1 shows the age structure of expellees in comparison with the native German population in West Germany in 1950. The age groups below 34 had a higher share among the expellee population. While among them only 7.5 percent were older than 65, this share was 9.8 percent among native Germans. The census of 1970 shows - as expected - that the age structure of the expellee population came closer to that of the German native population, after the reduction of annual immigration in the fifties.

Table 1: Occupational structure of expellees

	Share of all gainfully employed					
	Resettlers			Other Population		
	1939	1946	1950	1939	1946	1950
Agricultural professions	39,6	29,3	14,5	25,2	30	25,7
Industrial and technical profess., handicraft	33,2	37,5	52,4	37,8	36,3	40,7
Trade and transportation	17,4	11,8	14,0	17,9	16,7	18,4
Other professions 1)	9,8	21,4	19,1	19,1	17	15,2
Total	100	100	100	100	100	100

Data: Reichling, 1958, p.208

The occupational structure of expellees is shown in table 1. Before World War II there were considerable differences between economic and occupational structures in the so-called "Eastern territories" and in West Germany. The share of agriculture in production and employment was much higher in the East, while the share of industry was much lower. In the period 1939 to 1946 these structures changed slightly due to the war economy.

In the 1946 census the share of agricultural employees was approximately the same for the expellees and the rest of the West German population. But in case of the expellees their past occupation before the expulsion was recorded. Most of them had little chance to continue their former profession in West Germany. In 1950 the share of agricultural employees among expellees was only half of its 1946 value. Many farmers found a job in industry or in the services. There was a substantial restructuring in the occupation of expellees from agriculture to industry. The census in 1950 displayed that the share of industrial professions among expellees was even higher than among native West Germans. After World War II there was an acceleration in the secular shift from the primary to the secondary sector in most of Western European countries. In Germany this shift was supported by the occupational mobility of millions of expellees. More than 60 percent of the expellees changed their profession only in the period up to 1950. The high mobility of expellees reduced the individual cost of structural change for many native West Germans (Becker, 1992, p.35).

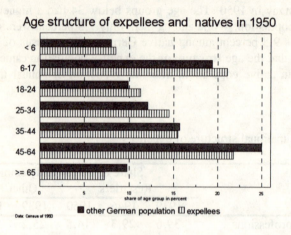

Chart 1

The reintegration of expellees in West Germany changed not only their occupational structure but also their occupational position. The share of employers and self-employed dropped from 20 percent before the war to 5 percent in 1950, while the share of employed laborers increased from 50 to 75 percent (Reichling, 1959, 210). Many expellees could not keep their social status after the expulsion (Albers, 1959, 446f; Luettinger, 1986, 1989; Becker, 1992).

The labor force participation of expellees was below the general average in West Germany. The main reason for that was not the labor supply behavior of expellees but a discouraged worker effect related to their high unemployment in the beginning of the fifties. Especially for older expellees a reintegration into the labor market seemed to be almost hopeless. Special pension regulations for them (*Entschädigungsrente, Kriegsschadenrente*) supported an earlier retirement. The share of pensioners in the age groups older than 50 was higher among expellees. In 1960 10 percent of the expellees in the age group from 51-60 were pensioners, while among native Germans this share was only 5 percent. In the age group between 61 and 73 44.5 percent of expellees were pensioners, but only 35 percent of the native Germans (Reichling, 1958, p.212). With the "German economic miracle" of the fifties and a decline of unemployment the labor force participation rate of expellees came closer to values reached by natives. At the census of 1970 it was almost identical with native labor force participation.

The social and demographic characteristics of current resettlers have similarities and differences as compared with the expellees of the fifties. The differences reflect partly the socio-economic development in the East-European countries of origin in the past forty years. To some degree they are also due to the fact, that this is now a voluntary migration and a self-selection of resettlers has an impact.

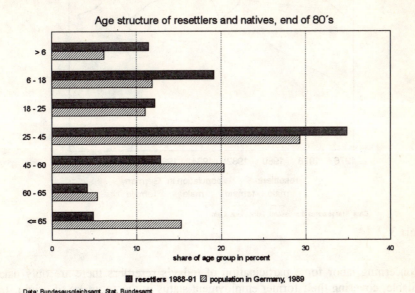

Data: Bundesausgleichsamt, Stat. Bundesamt

Chart 2

Chart 2 compares the age structure of the resettlers in the years 1988 to 1991 with the West German population in 1989. The difference is larger than in case of the expellees in the fifties. At first, the aging of the West German population in the past forty years was much faster than in East European countries. Secondly, the self-selection of resettlers has an effect here. But the age structure of resettlers will probably not remain that juvenile over the nineties, given the relative small size of the remaining German minority in Eastern Europe. One fourth of the potential resettlers of 1988 are already in Germany. During the first years of the current wave of resettlement the youngest and most mobile Germans came first. If resettlement continues, an increasing number of older people will follow their relatives who are already in Germany.

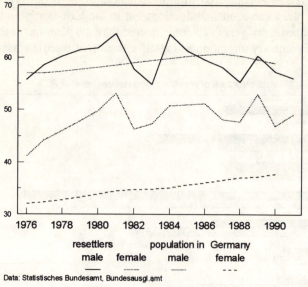

Chart 3

Concerning labor force participation of today's resettlers there are only data available, covering their former employment status in the countries of origin. In the period 1988-91 resettlers had a labor force participation rate of 52.4 at the moment of immigration. The (German and foreign) population in West Germany had a participation rate of 47.7 in 1990. Chart 3 shows the participation rate for both sexes from 1976 to 1990. Especially the female participation rate was higher among resettlers. It is highly doubtful if these differences have any significance for the labor market behavior of resettlers once they are in Germany. The formerly planned economies in their countries of origin are known for hidden unemployment. The high demand for labor and its inefficient use prevented open unemployment. Especially the labor force participation of women was publicly supported. These conditions are not given on the German labor market. Therefore it seems rather unprobable that the high labor force participation of female resettlers can be maintained (Hof, 1989, p.17). Other reasons for a higher participation rate, like a lower share of students in Eastern Europe and shorter times spent in the educational system do not apply in Germany. Older resettlers will have similar problems like older expellees in early fifties and partly retire early.

Table 2: Occupational structure of expellees, 1988-91

	Share of all gainfully employed		
	Resettlers 1988-91	West Germans, 1990 employed	unemployed
Agricultural professions	3,5	1,4	2,8
Mining profession	2,3	0,5	0,7
Industrial and technical profess., handicraft	46,7	36,1	37,9
Technical professions	6,7	7,0	3,8
Service professions	38,1	54,8	52,6
no category	2,8	0,2	2,2
Total	100	100	100

Data: Bundesausgleichsamt, Bundesanstalt für Arbeit

The occupational structure of todays resettlers is mainly influenced by the economic development in their countries of origin. Table 2 shows the occupational structure of resettlers according to main categories; chart 4 shows the share of single professions. The primary sector is overrepresented in the occupational structure of resettlers. This sector has experienced a decrease of employment in Germany over the past forty years (Dietz, 1988). It has unemployment rates above average today. Industrial occupations and handicraft are also overrepresented among resettlers. But the employment share of the secondary sector is declining for several years too. It had a net loss of 680 thousand jobs from 1976 to 1985 alone. Substantial changes in the structure of qualifications took place in the shrinking secondary sector. More than 1.1 million jobs without formal qualification has been lost, but 420 thousand more qualified jobs have been won (Tessaring, 1988, p.185). The picture gets more qualified when looking at single professions and branches. Electricians, fitters and mechanics are professions with good prospects on the German labor market which are overrepresented among resettlers. But is not valid for all manufacturing profession. Professions from the textile branch are also strongly represented among the resettlers. On the West Germany labor market there is a decreasing demand for these professions and consequently an unemployment higher than in average. The same goes for unskilled workers with no vocational training. This is the occupational group which is much represented among resettlers than in the German labor force.[5]

---

[5] The share of this group is perhaps overestimated in statistics, because it is a kind of a residual group.

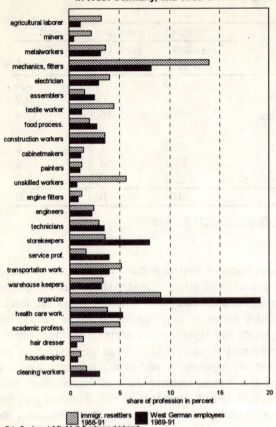

Chart 4

Service professions are with 31 percent clearly underrepresented among resettlers. In West Germany 55 percent of all employees belonged to this group in 1990. Some of these professions, like merchants, organizational profession and professions in the health care system had unemployment rates below the general average. They are underrepresented among resettlers.

The occupational structure of current resettlers does not allow a clear conclusion on good or bad prospects for their integration into the German labor market. Some resettlers came with professions which fitted in current needs of the labor market. But this is not the general pattern. Only 51 percent of resettlers came with professions with a below-average unemployment rate in Germany. On the other hand it will be difficult or impossible for many resettlers to work in their former professions here. Besides the profession, it will be qualification and command of German language which influence the chances for successful labor market integration.

It is very difficult to evaluate the qualifications of today's resettlers. About one third has no completed vocational training. 45 percent have a vocational training of at least two years (Blaschke, 1991, 57). More important than formal certificates are real qualifications. The formal acceptance of educational and vocational certificates are liberally regulated according to § 92 of the Federal Resettler Law (Bundesvertriebenengesetz). It is more oriented on maintaining the social status of resettlers than on real comparability with West German certificates. In many professions the qualifications of resettlers differ from actual requirements on the German labor market. This is not surprising, keeping in mind the technological gap between the East European countries of origin and West Germany. This gap is higher today than it was in the fifties. So we should expect that the qualification gap plays a more important role for today's resettlers than for the expellees of the fifties.

The German Federal Employment Office (*Bundesanstalt für Arbeit*) supports vocational qualification courses for resettlers. More than 40 percent of the resettlers immigrated between 1988 and 1991 entered such courses financed from public households. The share was decreasing.

The application of human capital brought by immigrants requires knowledge of native language. This is very important for qualified communicative professions, for example in large parts of the service sector. The command of German language was no problem for the expellees of the fifties. But in the past forty years the learning and sometimes the use of German language has been made difficult in the East European countries. Consequently about 80 percent of today's resettlers are in poor or no command of German language (Buttler, 1991, p.80). 88 percent of resettlers immigrated between 1988 and 1991 participated language courses over several months after arrival. These courses are also financed by the Federal Labor Office.

4 Integration into the German Labor Market

The German "economic miracle" of the fifties allowed the almost complete labor market integration of the expellees. But in the beginning of this period the unemployment rate of expellees was more than double of the native population's. While expellees had a share of 16 percent among population in Germany, they were represented with 34 percent among the unemployed (Becker, 1992, 12). There were several reasons for that. The occupational structure of expellees did not fit to the needs of the German labor market (See the preceding section). Former employers and self-employed expellees had no capital and should work as employees. These problems were reinforced by regional disproportions. Many expellees settled first in states with high unemployment, like Schleswig-Holstein, where expellees had a share of 56 percent among unemployed (Bethlehem, 1982, p.47). Unemployment among expellees was very high in agricultural professions and textile professions (Nellner, 1959, p.112).

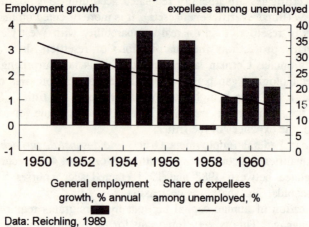

Chart 5

The unemployment of the immediate post-war period reached a peak in February 1950. Employment promotion measures, but more the boom induced by the war in Korea, brought a turning point. The expansion of employment in the booming fifties reduced the overall unemployment rate to 0.6 percent in 1961. There was a 2.5 percent annual growth rate of employment in the first half of the fifties (see chart 5). The West German economy experienced employment gains of this dimension later only in 1990 with the unification boom. The "economic miracle" of the fifties - and its effect on employment - was a unique phenomenon, reflecting the interaction of various factors. Among them were the favorable conditions created by the currency reform, the opportunity for export expansion and the huge internal demand for reconstruction. These factors together allowed the almost complete integration of expellees in the German labor market. Their unemployment rate leveled of with that of natives in 1961.

The regional mismatch-unemployment of expellees was also reduced thanks to their high spatial mobility. In the framework of four publicly organized and financed resettlement programs more than one million expellees changed their residence from one state to another. More than 250 thousand apartments were build to support these measures. The German public household spent two billion DM for the resettlement of expellees within Germany. Beside the publicly organized resettlements there were another 2.4 million removals on private initiative. Altogether 6.7 million expellees removed their residence within Germany, in statistical average almost every expellee.

The separate statistical coverage of unemployed expellees ended in 1961. Until the eighties the immigration of resettlers was to low to justify a separate unemployment statistic. Only with the current wave of resettler immigration labor market integration became a problem again. The branch structure of the German economy, its technological level, world market conditions, a highly regulated labor market, a well developed net of social services, persisting high levels of unemployment since the beginning of the seventies and the gradual integration of East- and West German labor markets are among those factors making a difference to the situation in the fifties. One could expect that the massive immigration of resettlers after 1988 could not be absorbed immediately by the German labor market.

The Federal Labor Office gives unemployment figures for resettlers who immigrated during the last five years. The number of those unemployed resettlers increased from 27 thousand in 1987 to 160 thousand in the end of 1990, but decreased than to 139.6 thousand in the end of 1991. If dividing the average number of unemployed resettlers by the number by the economically active resettlers immigrated in the last five years, an unemployment rate of 23.8 percent for resettlers would be the result.[6] A more accurate picture of current experiences with the labor market integration of resettlers can be gained from the Labor Force Account Balance (*LFAB*, *Arbeitskräfte-Gesamtrechnung*) for resettlers published by the Federal Labor Office.

The LFAB covers levels of different categories of the economically active and nonactive population and flows between them (Reyher/Bach, 1989). This approach allows to keep track, for example, how new immigration increased the account of unemployed resettlers or how language training reduced it. Unfortunately the change from the unemployed to the employed status is not unequivocal covered, since the respective account "Other economically active persons" includes not only the employed but also the discouraged workers. But since most resettlers are entitled to unemployment benefits, the share of discouraged workers in this account might be negligible. Therefore we can assume that actual entrance into employment is only little lower than the account "Other economically active persons" shows.

---

[6] From 1986 to 1991 706 thousand economically active resettlers came to Germany. There were 118 thousand resettlers in vocational or language training courses in 1991, not exposed to the risk of unemployment. They have been deducted. On the other side there were 139.8 thousand resettlers unemployed in the average of 1991. This calculation is of only limited comparability to overall unemployment rates as published by the Federal Labor Office.

Table 3: Labor Force Account Balance (LFAB) for resettlers, 1987-91, Changes and stocks in the account "unemployed", in 1000

	1987	1988	1989	1990	1991
Increase of labor force from immigration	41,4	104,4	213,8	206,4	116,3
absolute change		47,8	-109,0	-209,9	-160,0
Outflow to education programs	35,0	92,9	190,6	266,6	233,9
Inflow to education programs	28,4	46,1	131,7	261,5	259,5
Balance with education programs	-6,6	-46,8	-58,9	-5,1	25,6
Outflow to "other labor force"	19,8	16,0	113,2	173,4	162,3
Inflow from "other labor force"		6,6			
Balance with "other labor force"	-19,8	-9,4	-113,2	-173,4	-162,3
Initial stock fo unemployed	27,1	42,1	90,4	132,1	160,0
Final stock of unemployed	42,1	90,4	132,1	160,0	139,6
absolute change	15,0	48,3	41,7	27,9	-20,4

Data: Bundesanstalt f. Arbeit

Table 3 shows the movements between the account for registered unemployed resettlers and other accounts for the period 1987 to 1991. Negative values mean a reduction of unemployed resettlers due to transitions to the respective account. According to the concept of the LFAB all immigrating economically active resettlers are first entered to the account "unemployed". The inflow of this direction increased from 1987 to 1989. In 1990 the labor force participation rate of immigrating resettlers was slightly lower. With the new law on resettler promotion (*Aussiedlerförderungsgesetz*) the training programs were expanded. Consequently, these educational measures absorbed an increasing number of unemployed resettlers. This can be seen in the account "Balance to training courses". The highest absorption was in 1989 with 59 thousand persons. But the relief for the labor market is only of temporary nature. In 1990 it reached only five thousand, in 1991 there were more people leaving educational measures than entering them. The account "Other economically active persons" shows the entrance of unemployed resettlers into employment. It was relatively low in 1987 and 1988, but increased to 113 thousand in 1989. Obviously resettlers could participate the general employment expansion induced by the opening of East German markets. The entrance of resettlers into employment reached a peak in 1990 and decreased already in 1991 by 7 percent. The absolute decrease in the number of unemployed resettlers is more the result of reduced immigration than of increased absorption by the West German labor market.

Vertriebene and Aussiedler - The Immigration of Ethnic Germans   169

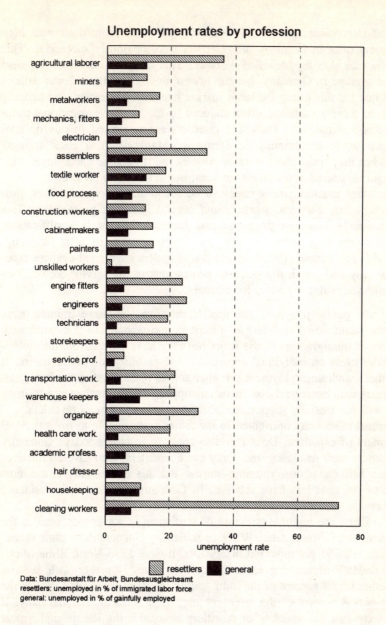

Chart 6

For which occupational groups among resettlers was the labor market integration easier, for which groups more difficult? Chart 6 shows profession specific unemployment rates for resettlers and the West German average. As expected, the unemployment rates of agricultural professions are above average. Good chances had electricians, fitters and mechanics. In some professions with high unemployment rates in Germany the resettlers were obviously successful. This seems to be true also for unskilled workers. This category has unemployment rates above average in Germany, but the lowest among resettlers. Some authors concluded that for this group the labor market integration is easier. But actually it seems to be more a statistical effect induced by the extensive vocational training programs for resettlers. Unskilled resettlers are registered in this occupational group while immigrating to Germany. Many of them enter training courses. When they finish these training courses and if they are unemployed they are no longer registered as unskilled workers, but in their new professions.

Above average unemployment rates can be found among organizational professions, engineers, chemical workers and several academic professions. This reflects obviously language problems and incompatibilities in qualification. These professions have unemployment rates below average in West Germany. Buttler (1991) and Gierse (1990) assume that resettlers have good chances especially with easy and physically oriented professions in the service sector. Surprisingly this seems not to be true for cleaners.

In sum, the public programs for qualification and language training have changed the occupational structure of resettlers substantially as compared with the moment of immigration. In the short run they have reduced the unemployment and the stress on individual adjustment and mobility for the resettlers. It might be that search unemployment is higher among resettlers than for immigrating foreigners who cannot rely on financial support. In the medium run training programs will substantially support the labor market integration of resettlers.

The regional mismatch contributed in the fifties considerable to the structural unemployment of expellees. Does this also apply to resettlers today? Generally they can choose their residence free. Only those resettlers, who have no relatives or any other help can choose rooming houses. But this applies only to a minority. Most of the resettlers have relatives in Germany and take their residence close to them.

As in the fifties the regional structure of settlement is not proportional to the population size of German states. While in Schleswig-Holstein there came six resettlers from 1988-91 per thousand inhabitants, it were 23 in North Rhine-Westfalia and Baden-Wuertemberg each. These two states, together with Bavaria count together for 67 percent of the immigrating resettlers from 1988-91. On the other side only 8 percent of the resettlers after 1991 went to East Germany. It does not seem that the majority of resettlers is considering the unemployment level of different states when choosing their first residence in Germany. But this can be rational job search behavior too, since the support of relatives could improve the chances of job search. Chart 7 shows the share of unemployed resettlers among all unemployed in different states. Since many resettlers come to North Rhine-Westfalia and this state has above average unemployment, a relative high share of unemployed resettlers could be expected. North Rhine-Westfalia has lost part of its attraction for resettlers in the past two years. A lower share of unemployed resettlers show Schleswig-Holstein, the Saar and Westberlin.

Chart 7

Some authors (among others Tiedtke, 1989) expected that the resettlers will move within a short time, adjusting their residence to labor market needs. Beginning with 1991 the Federal Administration Office (*Bundesverwaltungsamt*) is publishing data on the internal migration of resettlers who came in the last two years to Germany. According to these figures the internal migration of resettlers within the first two years in Germany is low. In 1991 there were only 3557 moves by resettlers from one state to another. One third of these moves were from East to West Germany.

5 Conclusions

The aim of this paper was to compare characteristics of expellees and resettlers and conditions for their labor market integration. Both groups were younger in their age structure than the German native population then. It has been argued that this might be less true for the resettlers of the next years. The labor force participation rate of resettlers in their countries of origin was very high, compared with West German levels. But it is not known how this will change while adjusting to the West German labor market. Today's resettlers are in an unfavorable starting position with regard to language competence and qualifications. This seems to be more a problem than in case of the expellees.

The current situation of the Federal Republic of Germany is better for the reception of resettlers than it was immediately after the war. It is possible to spend much more for the training of resettlers, than would have been possible in the fifties. The Federal Labor Office alone planned to spend three billion DM in 1992 for the integration of resettlers. The public welfare system is more developed today and gives instant security for the resettlers. The coincidence of the current wave of resettler immigration and the German unification created favorable conditions for the labor market integration.

While the current situation of the Federal Republic of Germany is better for the reception of resettlers this does not necessarily mean that a positive effect of this immigration to the economy can be expected. The positive effect the expellees had on the West German economy of the fifties was also the result of their enormous mobility. For today's resettlers (as for West German society as a whole) the stress for adjustment and mobility is lower than it was for the expellees in the fifties.

Optimistic authors expected two or three years ago a rapid labor market integration of resettlers. Available data show that this did not happen, although the general economic conditions were favorable. The labor market prospects of resettlers depend also from their success with qualification and language training. The structural change in West German labor demand will reduce the niche which allowed a quick integration of resettlers with low qualifications.

Considering the still high unemployment among recent resettlers, the costs for their training, for construction, specific welfare payments etc. it is obvious that the short term effect on public households is negative. A long term perspective has to consider all transfers over the life-cycle. It is methodological rather complex.

In the medium perspective the success of resettlers with their labor market integration is a key factor determining their effect on Germany´s public households. If resettlers reach unemployment rates below average after an initial phase, they could compensate the costs of their integration. But this seems rather unprobable. It has not been reached so far by expellees. The increasing link between the East German labor market in turmoil and the West German labor market does not make an optimistic scenario more probable. More than 500 thousand commuters from East Germany are an additional competition for the resettlers.

For the private sector, especially the employers, the increased immigration of resettlers was favorable. It helped to fill vacancies and overcome employment bottlenecks. The cost of integration of resettlers are external for the private sector. The relation between employed and unemployed resettlers is in this context not relevant. To a certain degree the increase of labor supply might exert a pressure in wages in the medium perspective. It might also decrease the pressure for labor saving investments.

References

Abelshauser, Werner: Der Lastenausgleich und die Eingliederung der Vertriebene und Flüchtlinge - Eine Skizze. In: Veröffentlichungen der historischen Kommisssion für Niedersachsen und Bremen, Nr. 38, Quellen und Untersuchungen zur Geschichte Niedersachsens nach 1945, Bd. 4, Flüchtlinge und Vertriebene in der westdeutschen Nachkriegsgeschichte, Rainer Schulze, Doris von der Brelie-Lewien, Helga Grebing (Hrsg.). Hildesheim

Albers, Willi: Die Eingliederung in volkswirtschaftlicher Sicht. In: Edding, F.; E. Lemberg (Hg.): Die Vertriebenen in Westdeutschland, Bd. 3, Kiel, 1959

Albers, Willi: Die soziale und wirtschaftliche Eingliederung von Aussiedlern und Übersiedlern. Wirtschaftsdienst; hrsg. vom HWWA-Institut für Wirtschaftsforschung-Hamburg; Hamburg; Verl. Weltarchiv; 70. 1990, Nr. 3; S. 139 - 145; 1990

Ambrosius, Gerold: Flüchtlinge und Vertriebene in der westdeutschen Wirtschaftsgeschichte: Methodische Überlegungen und forschungsrelevante Probleme. In: Veröffentlichungen der historischen Kommisssion für Niedersachsen und Bremen, Nr. 38, Quellen und Untersuchungen zur Geschichte Niedersachsens nach 1945, Bd. 4, Flüchtlinge und Vertriebene in der westdeutschen Nachkriegsgeschichte, Rainer Schulze, Doris von der Brelie-Lewien, Helga Grebing (Hrsg.). Hildesheim

Bach, H. U.; Brinkmann, Ch.; Kohler, H.; Spitznagel, E.: Zur Arbeitsmarktentwicklung 1990/1991 im vereinigten Deutschland. Mitteilungen aus der Arbeitsmarkt- und Berufsforschung, 23 Jg., Heft 4, 1990, S. 455-473

Bach, H.-U.; Bogai, Dieter; Kohler, Hans u.a.: Der Arbeitsmarkt 1991 und 1992 in der Bundesrepublik Deutschland. Mitteilungen aus der Arbeitsmarkt- und Berufsforschung, 24. Jg., Heft 4, 1991, S. 621-634

Bade, Klaus J.: Neue Heimat im Westen: Vertriebene, Flüchtlinge, Aussiedler. Münster: 1990

Bals, Christel: Aussiedler - Erneut ein räumliches Problem? Informationen zur Raumentwicklung, Bonn-Bad Godesberg, Heft 5, 1989, S. 305 ff.

Becker, Rolf: Flüchtlinge, Vertriebene, Aus- und Übersiedler. Einwanderung, Integration und berufliche Mobilität im Lebenslauf. Berlin: 1992

Bethlehem, Siegfried: Heimatvertreibung, DDR-Flucht, Gastarbeiterzuwanderung. Stuttgart, Klett-Cotta, 1982

Blaschke, D.: Sozialbilanz der Aussiedlung in den 80er und 90er Jahren. In: Baumeister, H.-P. (Hrsg.): Integration von Vertriebenen, Weinheim, 1991, S. 35-77

Blaschke, Dieter: Aussiedler - eine Problemskizze aus der Sicht der Arbeitsmarkt- und Berufsforschung. Arbeit und Sozialpolitik; Baden-Baden; Lutzeyer; 43. 1989, H. 8/9; S. 238 - 245 : Ill., zahlr. statist. Übersichten; 1989

Blaschke, Dieter: Aussiedler und Übersiedler auf dem bundesdeutschen Arbeitsmarkt. Wirtschaftsdienst; hrsg. vom <u>HWWA-Institut für Wirtschaftsforschung-Hamburg</u>; Hamburg; Verl. Weltarchiv; 70. 1990, Nr. 5; S. 256 - 263

Buttler, Friedrich: Aussiedler - Herausforderungen an das Bildungssystem und den Arbeitsmarkt, Ansatzpunkte für Problemlösungen. In: Sikora, Joachim (Hrsg.): <u>Aussiedler als Herausforderung und Auftrag für die deutsche Gesellschaft</u>. Bad Honnef, 1991

Buttler, Günter; Winterstein, Helmut; Jaeger, Norbert: Aussiedler - ein Gewinn oder Verlust für das System der Sozialen Sicherung? <u>Arbeit und Sozialpolitik;</u> Baden-Baden; Lutzeyer; 43. 1989, H. 8/9; S. 232 - 237

Die Integration deutscher Aussiedler - Perspektiven für die Bundesrepublik Deutschland. Köln, <u>Institut der deutschen Wirtschaft</u>, 1989

Dietz, Frido: Strukturwandel auf dem Arbeitsmarkt. <u>Mitteilungen aus der Arbeitsmarkt- und Berufsforschung,</u> 21. Jg., Heft 1, 1988, S. 115-152

Edding, Friedrich: Die Flüchtlinge als Belastung und Antrieb der westdeutschen Wirtschaft. <u>Kieler Studien, Forschungsberichte des Instituts für Weltwirtschaft an der Universität Kiel</u>, Fritz Bade (Hrsg.), Nr. 12

Fleischer, Henning; Proebsting, Helmut: Aussiedler und Übersiedler - Zahlenmäßige Entwicklung und Struktur. <u>Wirtschaft und Statistik,</u> 9/89

Frantzioch, M.: <u>Die Vertriebenen. Hemmnisse, Antriebskräfte und Wege ihrer Integration in der Bundesrepublik Deutschland.</u> Berlin: 1987

Frantzioch, Marion: Die Vertriebenen - Hemmnisse, Antriebskräfte und Wege ihrer Integration in der Bundesrepublik Deutschland. In: <u>Schriften zur Kultursoziologie</u>, Stagl, Justin (Hg.), Band 9, Berlin: Dietrich Reimer Verlag

Gesetz über die Angelegenheiten der Vertriebenen und Flüchtlinge (Bundesvertriebenengesetz) - <u>BVFG. Bundesgesetzblatt,</u> Jahrgang 1953, Teil I

Gesetz zur Regelung des Aufnahmeverfahrens für Aussiedler (Aussiedleraufnahmegesetz - AAG). <u>Bundesgesetzblatt, Nr. 32,</u> Bonn, den 30. Juni 1990

Gierse, Matthias: Kurzfristige Arbeitsmarktwirkungen des Zustroms von Aus- und Übersiedlern. <u>RWI-Mitteilungen,</u> Jg. 41 (1990), S. 153-167

Hof, Bernd: Aussiedler, Asylbewerber und die Entwicklung des Arbeitskräfteangebots bis 1995. <u>iw-trends, Institut der deutschen Wirtschaft</u>, 15(4), 1988

Hof, Bernd: Modellierung zu den Auswirkungen einer verstärkten Aussiedler-Zuwanderung auf Bevölkerung, Wirtschaftswachstum und Arbeitsmarkt. In: <u>Die Integration deutscher Aussiedler - Perspektiven für die Bundesrepublik Deutschland</u>; Institut der deutschen Wirtschaft, Köln, 1989

Jolles, H.: <u>Zur Soziologie der Heimatvertriebenen und Flüchtlinge</u>. Köln/Berlin: 1965

Kleinert, Uwe: Die Flüchtlinge als Arbeitskräfte - zur Eingliederung der Flüchtlinge in Nordrhein-Westfalen nach 1945. in: <u>Neue Heimat im Westen: Vertriebene, Flüchtlinge, Aussiedler;</u> hrsg. von Klaus Bade, Westfälischer Heimatbund, Münster 1990

Leciejewski, Klaus: Zur wirtschaftlichen Eingliederung der Aussiedler. In: <u>Aus Politik und Zeitgeschichte,</u> Beilage zur Wochenzeitung Das Parlament, B3/90

Lemberg, E.; Edding, F. (Hrsg.): <u>Die Vertriebenen in Deutschland.</u> 3 Bände. Kiel: 1959

Luettinger, P.: Der Mythos der schnellen Integration. Eine empirische Untersuchung zur Integration der Vertriebenen und Flüchtlinge in der Bundesrepublik Deutschland bis 1971. <u>Zeitschrift für Soziologie</u>, 15 Jg., 1986, S. 20-36

Luettinger, P.: <u>Integration der Vertriebenen</u>. Frankfurt a. M.: 1989

Nellner, Werner: Grundlagen und Hauptergebnisse der Statistik. In: <u>Die Vertriebenen in Westdeutschland</u>, Eugen Lemberg, Friedrich Edding (Hrsg.), Kiel: Ferdinand Hirt

Projektgruppe Sonderprogramm Aussiedler: Sonderprogramm zur Eingliederung der Aussiedler - <u>Beschluß der Bundesregierung vom 31.08.1988</u>. Bundesminister des Innern, VtK I 4 - 933 900 - 2/3

Reichling, Gerhard: Die deutschen Vertriebenen in Zahlen - Teil II - 40 Jahre Eingliederung in der Bundesrepublik Deutschland. <u>Kulturstiftung der deutschen Vertriebenen</u>, Bonn, Meckenheim: Warlich Druck

Reichling, Gerhard: Die deutschen Vertriebenen in Zahlen, Teil 1 - Umsiedler, Verschleppte, Vertriebnen, Aussiedler 1940 - 1985. <u>Kulturstiftung der deutschen Vertriebenen</u>, Bonn, Meckenheim: Warlich Druck

Reichling, Gerhard: Die Heimatvertriebenen im Spiegel der Statistik. In: <u>Schriften des Vereins für Sozialpolitik, Gesellschaft für Wirtschafts- und Sozialwissenschaften</u>, Neue Folge Band 6/III, Untersuchungen zum deutschen Flüchtlingsproblem, Pfister, Bernhard (Hg.), Berlin: Duncker & Humboldt

Reyher, Lutz; Bach, Hans-Uwe: Der Potential-Effekt der Zuwanderungen - Eine Arbeitskräfte-Gesamtrechnung für Aus- und Übersiedler. <u>Mitteilungen aus der Arbeitsmarkt- und Berufsforschung</u>, Nr. 4, 22. Jg., 1989, S. 468-471

Schulze, R.; Brelie-Lewien, D. v.d.; Grebing, H. (Hrsg.): <u>Flüchtlinge und Vertriebene in der westdeutschen Nachkriegsgeschichte</u>. Hildesheim: 1987

Sikora, Joachim (Hrsg.): <u>Aussiedler als Herausforderung und Auftrag für die deutsche Gesellschaft</u>. Bad Honnef, 1991.

Sprink, Joachim; Hellmann, Wolfgang: Finanzielle Belastung oder ökonomisches Potential - Regional unterschiedliche Konsequenzen des Aussiedlerzustroms. <u>Informationen zur Raumentwicklung</u>, Bonn-Bad Godesberg, Heft 5, 1989, S. 323-329

Statistisches Bundesamt: Bevölkerung nach dem Wohnsitz am 1. Sep. 1939 und nach dem Besitz eines Bundesvertriebenen- oder Bundesflüchtlingsausweises. Ergebnisse einer Sonderauszählung aus der Mikrozensus-Erhebung vom Oktober 1957 . <u>Wirtschaft und Statistik,</u> Heft 7, Stuttgart: S-. 409-412

Statistisches Bundesamt: Vertriebene und Deutsche aus der sowjetischen Besatzungszone und dem Sowjetsektor von Berlin am 6. Juni 1961 nach dem Jahr des Zuzugs in das Bundesgebiet. Ergebnisse der Volkszählung am 6. Juni 1961. <u>Wirtschaft und Statistik</u>, Heft 1, Stuttgart: S. 34-37

Statistisches Bundesamt: Volks- und Berufszählung vom 6. Juni 1961 - Heft 6 - Vertriebene und Deutsche aus der SBZ - <u>Verteilung und Struktur. Fachserie A - Bevölkerung und Kultur</u>, W. Kohlhammer GMBH, Stuttgart und Mainz, 1961

Taureg, Ulrich; Weiß, Thomas: Der kurzfristige Nachfrageimpuls des Zustroms von Aus- und Übersiedlern. <u>RWI-Mitteilungen</u>, Jg. 41 (1990), S. 169-181

Tessaring, Manfred: Arbeitslosigkeit, Beschäftigung und Qualifikation: Ein Rück- und Ausblick. <u>Mitteilungen aus der Arbeitsmarkt- und Berufsforschung</u>, 22 Jg., Heft 2, 1988

Tiedtke, Klaus-Peter: Die deutschen Aussiedler - Hintergründe, Fakten und Perspektiven der Aussiedlung und der Eingliederung. <u>Informationen zur Raumentwicklung</u>, Bonn-Bad Godesberg, Heft 5, 1989, S. 343-352

von Hamm, Ludwig: Ein integrierter Ansatz zur Untersuchung der Aussiedlerzuwanderung. <u>Informationen zur Raumentwicklung</u>, Bonn-Bad Godesberg, Heft 5, 1989, S. 377 ff.

Winterstein, Helmut: Aussiedler - Auswirkungen auf das Soziale Sicherungssystem. In: Sikora, Joachim (Hrsg.): <u>Aussiedler als Herausforderung und Auftrag für die deutsche Gesellschaft</u>. Bad Honnef, 1991

Studies in Contemporary Economics

B. Hamminga, Neoclassical Theory Structure and Theory Development. IX, 174 pages. 1983.

J. Dermine, Pricing Policies of Financial Intermediaries. VII, 174 pages. 1984.

Economic Consequences of Population Change in Industrialized Countries. Proceedings. 1983. Edited by G. Steinmann. X, 415 pages. 1984.

Problems of Advanced Economies. Proceedings, 1982. Edited by N. Miyawaki. VI, 319 pages. 1984.

Studies in Labor Market Dynamics. Proceedings, 1982. Edited by G. R. Neumann and N. C. Westergard-Nielsen. X, 285 pages. 1985.

A. Pfingsten, The Measurement of Tax Progression. VI, 131 pages. 1986.

Causes of Contemporary Stagnation. Proceedings, 1984. Edited by H. Frisch and B. Gahlen. IX, 216 pages. 1986.

O. Flaaten, The Economics of Multispecies Harvesting. VII, 162 pages. 1988.

D. Laussel, W. Marois, A. Soubeyran, (Eds.), Monetary Theory and Policy. Proceedings, 1987. XVIII, 383 pages. 1988.

G. Rubel, Factors Determining External Debt. VI, 264 pages. 1988.

B. C. J. van Velthoven, The Endogenization of Government Behaviour in Macroeconomic Models. XI, 367 pages. 1989.

A. Wenig, K. F. Zimmermann (Eds.) 3, Demographic Change and Economic Development. XII, 325 pages. 1989.

J. K. Brunner, Theory of Equitable Taxation. VIII, 217 pages. 1989.

E. van Imhoff, Optimal Economic Growth and Non-Stable Population. IX, 218 pages. 1989.

P. S. A. Renaud, Applied Political Economic Modelling. XII, 242 pages. 1989.

H. König (Ed.), Economics of Wage Determination. XI, 373 pages. 1990.

C. Dagum, M. Zenga (Eds.) Income and Wealth Distribution, Inequality and Poverty. Proceedings, XIII, 415 pages. 1990.

A. J. H. C. Schram, Voter Behavior in Economic Perspective. X, 274 pages. 1991.

J. B. Woittiez, Modelling and Empirical Evaluation of Labour Supply Behaviour. VI, 232 pages. 1991.

R. Arnason, T. Bjorndal (Eds.), Essays on the Economics of Migratory Fish Stocks. VIII, 197 pages. 1991.

Ch. Czerkawski, Theoretical and Policy-Oriented Aspects of the External Debt Economics. VII, 150 pages. 1991.

D. Stern, J. M. M. Ritzen (Eds.), Market Failure in Training? VII, 233 pages. 1991.

M. Savioz, New Issues in the Theory of Investment. XVI, 216 pages. 1992.

W. Franz (Ed.) Structural Unemployment. X, 132 pages. 1992.

N. Blattner, H. Genberg, A. Swoboda, (Eds.), Competitiveness in Banking. VIII, 315 pages. 1992.

M. Carlberg, Monetary and Fiscal Dynamics. VIII, 194 pages. 1992.

H.-J. Wagener, On the Theory and Policy of Systemic Change. VIII, 234 pages. 1993.

E. Wurzel, An Econometric Analysis of Individual Unemployment Duration in West Germany. V, 244 pages. 1993.

W. Gebauer, Foundations of European Central Bank Policy. VI, 258 pages. 1993.

G. de Wit, Determinants of Self-employment. XII, 194 pages. 1993.

W. Smolny, Dynamic Factor Demand in a Rationing Context. VIII, 242 pages. 1993.

A. Haufler, Commodity Tax Harmonization in the European Community. XIV, 216 pages. 1993.

N. Blattner, H. Genberg, A. Swoboda (Eds.), Banking in Switzerland. VIII, 330 pages. 1993.

H.-J. Wagener (Ed.), The Political Economy of Transformation. VIII, 242 pages. 1994.

G. Steinmann, R. E. Ulrich (Eds.), The Economic Consequences of Immigration to Germany. X, 178 pages. 1994.

Springer-Verlag and the Environment

We at Springer-Verlag firmly believe that an international science publisher has a special obligation to the environment, and our corporate policies consistently reflect this conviction.

We also expect our business partners – paper mills, printers, packaging manufacturers, etc. – to commit themselves to using environmentally friendly materials and production processes.

The paper in this book is made from low- or no-chlorine pulp and is acid free, in conformance with international standards for paper permanency.

Printing: Weihert-Druck GmbH, Darmstadt
Binding: Theo Gansert Buchbinderei GmbH, Weinheim